Understanding

To Kill a
Mockingbird

New and future titles in the Understanding Great Literature series include:

Understanding

To Kill a
Mockingbird

UNDERSTANDING GREAT LITERATURE

Catherine Bernard

**LUCENT
BOOKS** ®

THOMSON
————— ✳ —————™
GALE

San Diego • Detroit • New York • San Francisco • Cleveland
New Haven, Conn. • Waterville, Maine • London • Munich

THOMSON

™

GALE

On cover: In the film version of *To Kill a Mockingbird*, lawyer Atticus Finch, played by Gregory Peck, defends Tom Robinson (Brock Peters), a black man unjustly accused of raping a white woman.

For more information, contact
Lucent Books
27500 Drake Rd.
Farmington Hills, MI 48331-3535
Or you can visit our Internet site at http://www.gale.com

LIBRARY OF CONGRESS CATALOGING-IN-PUBLICATION DATA

Bernard, Catherine.
    Understanding to kill a mockingbird / by Catherine Bernard.
        p. cm. — (Understanding Great Literature)
    Summary: An introduction to Harper Lee's famous novel, "To Kill a Mockingbird," discussing the author's life, the historical context of the novel, its plot, themes, characters, literary criticism, and pertinence for today's audiences.
    Includes bibliographical references (p.) and index.
    ISBN 1-56006-860-4 (alk. paper)
    1. Lee, Harper. To kill a mockingbird — Juvenile literature. [1. Lee, Harper. To kill a mockingbird. 2. American literature — History and criticism.] I. Title. II. Series.
    PS3562.E353T63 2003
    813'.54—dc21

                                                                        2002156251

Contents

FOREWORD

"**E**xcept for a living man, there is nothing more wonderful than a book!" wrote the widely respected nineteenth-century teacher and writer Charles Kingsley. A book, he continued, "is a message to us from human souls we never saw. And yet these [books] arouse us, terrify us, teach us, comfort us, open our hearts to us as brothers." There are many different kinds of books, of course; and Kingsley was referring mainly to those containing literature—novels, plays, short stories, poems, and so on. In particular, he had in mind those works of literature that were and remain widely popular with readers of all ages and from many walks of life.

Such popularity might be based on one or several factors. On the one hand, a book might be read and studied by people in generation after generation because it is a literary classic, with characters and themes of universal relevance and appeal. Homer's epic poems, the *Iliad* and the *Odyssey*, Chaucer's *Canterbury Tales*, Shakespeare's *Hamlet* and *Romeo and Juliet*, and Dickens's *A Christmas Carol* fall into this category. Some popular books, on the other hand, are more controversial. Mark Twain's *Huckleberry Finn* and J.D. Salinger's *The Catcher in the Rye*, for instance, have their legions of devoted fans who see them as great literature; while others view them as less than worthy because of their racial depictions, profanity, or other factors.

Still another category of popular literature includes realistic modern fiction, including novels such as Robert Cormier's *I Am the Cheese* and S.E. Hinton's *The Outsiders*. Their keen social insights and sharp character portrayals have consistently

6

reached out to and captured the imaginations of many teenagers and young adults; and for this reason they are often assigned and studied in schools.

These and other similar works have become the "old standards" of the literary scene. They are the ones that people most often read, discuss, and study; and each has, by virtue of its content, critical success, or just plain longevity, earned the right to be the subject of a book examining its content. (Some, of course, like the *Iliad* and *Hamlet*, have been the subjects of numerous books already; but their literary stature is so lofty that there can never be too many books about them!) For millions of readers and students in one generation after another, each of these works becomes, in a sense, an adventure in appreciation, enjoyment, and learning.

The main purpose of Lucent's Understanding Great Literature series is to aid the reader in that ongoing literary adventure. Each volume in the series focuses on a single literary work that a majority of critics and teachers view as a classic and/or that is widely studied and discussed in schools. A typical volume first tells why the work in question is important. Then follow detailed overviews of the author's life, the work's historical background, its plot, its characters, and its themes. Numerous quotes from the work, as well as by critics and other experts, are interspersed throughout and carefully documented with footnotes for those who wish to pursue further research. Also included is a list of ideas for essays and other student projects relating to the work, an appendix of literary criticisms and analyses by noted scholars, and a comprehensive annotated bibliography.

The great nineteenth-century American poet Henry David Thoreau once quipped: "Read the best books first, or you may not have a chance to read them at all." For those who are reading or about to read the "best books" in the literary canon, the comprehensive, thorough, and thoughtful volumes of the Understanding Great Literature series are indispensable guides and sources of enrichment.

Enduring Appeal

To *Kill a Mockingbird*, by Harper Lee, published in 1960, is one of the most widely read novels of the last fifty years. Within only a year of its publication, it had sold over half a million copies and had been translated in ten languages. By 1982, those figures ballooned to an astonishing 15 million sold and forty different translations. Many readers are first introduced to the novel in high school, where it is consistently taught in English courses. According to *A Study of Book-Length Works Taught in High School English Courses*, the novel has always ranked as one of the ten most frequently assigned books in high school classrooms since its publication in 1960.

Perhaps more important than the quantities sold, however, is the influence the book has had on its readers. Lee's novel, set in 1930s Alabama, revolves around the blatantly unjust trial of a black man named Tom Robinson and the efforts of Atticus Finch, a white lawyer, to defend him. Through it all, Atticus's daughter Scout, the narrator, must grapple with what her father's actions mean within a time and place where most members of her community believe African Americans to be inherently less important than white people. For many readers, Tom Robinson's trial is an eye-opener to racial prejudice. A 1991 survey sponsored by the Book of the Month Club and the Library of Congress's Center for the Book found that *To*

Kill a Mockingbird was second only to the Bible as the book that most made a difference in people's lives.

While racial prejudice is certainly at the forefront of the story, Lee also offers readers lessons on a much broader range of issues, thus adding to its enduring appeal. The story is told from the point of view of an adult Scout as she looks back on the events of her childhood as perceived by her six- to eight-year-old self. As she matures, she must come to new understandings about the prejudices of a small Southern community, about the nature of good and evil, and about compassion, hatred, and justice. She also learns about the importance of not judging people by what makes them different, not only through Tom Robinson, but also through her mysterious neighbor, Boo Radley. Scout tells her story as honestly as possible, giving the novel a sense of childlike innocence. Difficult, complex concepts are presented objectively, rather than being preached overtly to the reader. In other words, Lee deliberately peppers her story with powerful themes and lessons, but she also allows the reader to reach his or her own conclusions about them.

Being told through the eyes of a young girl, the story is also very much the story of childhood and growing up. Interspersed with the trial are episodes of childhood games, afternoon play, and first days at school. The novel appeals to readers' sense of nostalgia as they read of Scout playing with her brother Jem and her friend Dill, as well as the way they interact with the eccentric cast of adults in their lives.

Despite the overwhelming popularity of the novel, scholars have largely ignored it. While a similarly themed book, Mark Twain's *Huckleberry Finn*, has been the subject of countless studies, only a handful of articles and one full-length book have been devoted to Lee's novel. Reviewers, too, were not universally impressed with *To Kill a Mockingbird* when it came out in 1960. Phoebe Adams of the *Atlantic Monthly* wrote that the point of view "is frankly and completely impossible."[1] Others felt Lee's depiction of life in a small Southern town was overly sentimental.

Since 1960, most pieces written on *To Kill a Mockingbird* focus not on the novel, but on its elusive author. Lee not only never wrote another novel, but, with the exception of three short magazine articles, never published anything again. Adding to the aura of mystery that surrounds her is the fact that she has chosen to live her life outside the public eye. She lives in near obscurity, splitting her time between New York City and Monroeville, Alabama, the small town where she grew up. She refuses nearly all interviews and public speaking appearances. Those few she does grant are always on the condition that she not be quoted directly.

In the end, however, while Lee may choose not to speak directly to readers, her novel has spoken to generations of readers for over forty years. *To Kill a Mockingbird* is a simple story about complicated issues. While racism may no longer be as blatant as it was in the 1930s, when the book is set, or the 1950s, when it was written, it still certainly exists on many levels today. People will sometimes judge those who are different from themselves, evil will sometimes coexist with good, and children will sometimes be forced into new recognitions of their world as they grow into adults. For these reasons and many more, the lessons of *To Kill a Mockingbird* will remain important and the novel will continue to endure.

CHAPTER ONE

The Life of Harper Lee

D espite the immense interest generated by *To Kill a Mockingbird*, little is known about the novel's Pulitzer prize–winning author. After the publication of her first and only novel, Harper Lee retreated entirely from the limelight, refusing nearly all interviews and public appearances. In the 1995 foreword to the novel, Lee explained her absence from the public eye by simply writing, "I am still alive, although very quiet."[2] In order to learn more about the elusive author's life, some people have turned to the very novel that made Lee famous. Indeed, there are numerous similarities between Lee's life and that of Scout Finch, the novel's protagonist, although Lee has always maintained that *To Kill a Mockingbird* is not based on her own life. Other people rely on secondhand stories about Lee growing up, as remembered by childhood acquaintances and residents of her hometown in Alabama. Still others turn to the scant handful of interviews Lee has granted in the nearly forty-five years since the novel's publication. While the story of Lee's life can be pieced together from these various sources, gaps will always exist as long as the author remains silent.

Growing Up in Alabama

Harper Lee, born Nelle Harper Lee in 1926, grew up in the sleepy, Southern town of Monroeville, Alabama. According to resident Marianne Moates, Monroeville is "a small town with tree-lined sidewalks, a downtown square, and friendly people who lived in houses with big front porches."[3] Harper Lee, or Nelle as friends and family know her, spent her entire childhood in Monroeville and later used it as the model for the fictional town of Maycomb, the setting of *To Kill a Mockingbird*.

Lee was the youngest child of attorney Amasa C. Lee and his wife Frances Finch Cunningham Lee. Amasa Lee was a prominent lawyer and a well-respected member of his community. In addition to practicing law, he served in the state legislature from 1926 to 1938 and even edited the local weekly newspaper, the *Monroe Journal*, from 1929 to 1947. According to Marie Rudisill, the Lees' neighbor, Mr. Lee was

Harper Lee's Origins

"a tall, angular man, detached, not particularly friendly, especially with children."[4] Rudisill goes on to say that most children were rather intimidated by Mr. Lee's formal manner. He loved crossword puzzles and always stressed the importance of education and learning to his children. While her father may not have been overly demonstrative, Nelle idolized him nonetheless. Her unwavering admiration eventually took the shape of Atticus Finch, the dignified, moral lawyer she admittedly based on her own father.

Frances, Amasa's wife, came from an old Southern family in Virginia. She was trained as a classical pianist and chose to spend most of her days practicing. The housework was left primarily to the Lees' black housekeeper, Haddy. Frances was a kind, caring mother, but according to biographer Marianne

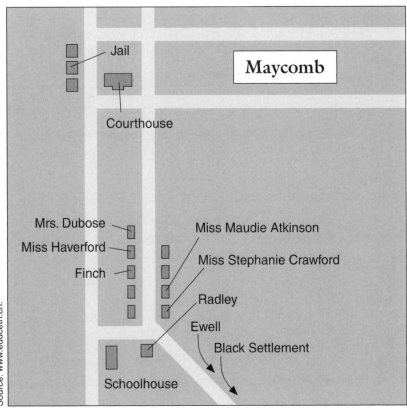

Source: www.educeth.ch.

Moates was "considered eccentric, judged by her habit of arising around 2:00 A.M., sitting before the big upright piano, and banging out tunes that in the summer months could be heard all the way to the downtown square."[5]

Nelle was the youngest of the Lees' four children. The firstborn, a son, died shortly after birth. The oldest girl, Alice, was already in high school by the time Nelle was born. Alice was studious, smart, and considered by many to be her father's favorite. Louise was born a few years after Alice. She was prim, proper, and relatively quiet. Nelle, the youngest, was the most energetic and rambunctious of the Lee children.

Nelle's family and the town of Monroeville offered her the makings of a happy childhood, filled with typical games and adventures. In one of her rare interviews, Lee described her early years in some detail:

> This was my childhood: If I went to a film once a month it was pretty good for me, and for all children like me. We had to use our own devices in our play, for our entertainment. We didn't have much money. Nobody had any money. We didn't have toys, nothing was done for us, so the result was that we lived in our imagination most of the time. We devised things; we were readers, and we would transfer everything we had seen on the printed page to the backyard in the form of high drama.[6]

Truman Capote and the "Queen of the Tomboys"

Lee's closest childhood friend was a boy named Truman Capote, who would also grow up to be a very famous writer. Capote did not live in Monroeville, but like Dill Harris, the character Lee based on Capote, he would spend his summers there, visiting relatives. Capote and Lee's childhood relationship is, in fact, similar in many ways to the fictional relationship between Dill and Scout. Like Dill, Capote was two years older than Nelle but was nearly the same size as she.

Despite his small size, he seemed old for his age, often employing a vocabulary more suited for an adult than a child. Capote was fond of using his gift for words to make up elaborate stories and tall tales, also much like Dill. In one final similarity to Dill, Capote often found himself on the losing end of a fistfight during the times he angered his high-spirited friend Nelle.

Like Scout from *To Kill a Mockingbird*, Nelle was very much a feisty tomboy. She never liked to wear dresses and was quick to settle arguments with her fists. Lucky for

As a youngster, author Harper Lee was a spirited tomboy.

her, she was so good at fighting that she could take on most of the boys her age—a trait that led former classmate George Thomas Jones to nickname her the "Queen of the Tomboys."[7] Neighbor Marie Rudisill, who was also Capote's aunt, remembers Lee in similar terms in a description that bears striking resemblance to Scout Finch:

> Nelle . . . grew up a high-strung, boisterous, noisy tomboy. She much preferred overalls to dresses. In fact, a dress on the young Nelle would have been as out of place as a silk hat on a hog's head. She was a real fighter and could lick most of the boys her own

age in town. Truman learned quickly never to get into a quarrel with Nelle. She always ended up flinging him to the ground and hopping up and down on him like an angry bantam rooster.[8]

Both Lee and Capote were unusually intelligent for their age, and they often put their wildly imaginative minds to use to create all kinds of games. They collected insects, played marbles, sold homemade lemonade, read old magazines, and flew kites. Rudisill claimed that the most likely place to find the children was "under the big yellow rosebushes in the backyard with an ancient Underwood typewriter that Mr. Lee had given them. They loved to play at being writers."[9]

Capote liked to say he was the one who first encouraged Lee to write. In an interview with journalist Gloria Steinem, he contended: "When we were children, I had a typewriter and worked every day in a little room I used as an office. I convinced [Lee] she ought to write, too, so we would work there each day for two or three hours. She didn't really want to, but I held her to it. We kept to that routine for quite a long time."[10]

Leaving Alabama

While her summers were spent with Capote, her school years were spent in Monroeville public schools. The Lees' house was only two blocks from the elementary school, so Nelle walked to class nearly every day. According to Marianne Moates, a Capote biographer, "one of the big oak trees on the school grounds" that Nelle would pass was "the tree where Boo Radley had hidden trinkets for Scout and Jem in *To Kill a Mockingbird*."[11] Not much is known of Nelle's education in Monroeville, except that she was generally bored with her classes.

After graduating high school, Lee enrolled in Huntingdon College, a women's college in nearby Montgomery, Alabama. A year later, she transferred to the University of Alabama, where she studied law for four years; she planned to be an attorney like her father. While there, she also wrote for several student publications, including a humor magazine. She also wrote a one-act play satirizing the Ku Klux Klan.

The last leg of Lee's studies included a semester as an exchange student at Oxford University in England. However, she dropped out of the University of Alabama six months before she obtained her degree. In 1950, Lee decided to move to New York City to become a writer, rather than be a lawyer in the South. Two years earlier, in 1948, her old friend Truman Capote, with whom she had stayed very close, published his first novel, *Other Voices, Other Rooms*, to much acclaim. Some people speculate that Capote's early literary success inspired Lee to pursue her own growing interest in writing.

Once in New York, however, Lee's literary career did not immediately take off. She spent her days working as an airline reservation clerk, refusing to write even a letter during work for fear of drying up her creativity. In the evenings, she would return to her tiny apartment to write as much as she could.

A photo of New York City in 1949. Intent on pursuing a career as a writer, Lee moved to this center of American culture in 1950.

Soon after moving to New York, she had begun working on the novel that would later become *To Kill a Mockingbird*. Once removed from her tiny hometown, Lee was able to reflect on life in the South through her writing. Although she had decided against a career as an attorney, the law still served as a major influence on her work and provided inspiration for her novel. However, despite the rigorous schedule Lee had laid out for herself and her self-imposed ban against daytime writing, Lee was simply unable to complete her novel while having to work full-time.

In December 1956, a group of Lee's friends surprised her with a wonderful gift—they had collected enough money to allow her to take a year off from work and devote herself full-time to writing. Lee was overwhelmed by her friends' kindness. She later wrote about their incredible gesture in a short magazine article:

> They wanted to give me a full, fair chance to learn my craft, free from the harassments of a regular job. Would I accept their gift? There were no strings at all. Please accept, with their love. . . . A full, fair chance for a new life. Not given me by an act of generosity, but by an act of love. *Our faith in you* was really all I had heard them say. I would do my best not to fail them.[12]

To Kill a Mockingbird

The additional time to write indeed helped Lee. By 1957, she had a first draft of *To Kill a Mockingbird* ready, which she submitted to J.B. Lippincott, a famous publishing house in New York. An editor named Tay Hohoff saw promise in the story, but believed it still needed a good deal of work. In a special 1960 introduction to the novel, Hohoff explained:

> There were many things wrong about it. It was more a collection of short stories than a true novel. And—

and yet, there was also life. It was real. The people walked solidly on the pages; they could be seen and heard and felt. No editorial department willingly lets that kind of book out of its hands. So we had asked to meet Miss Lee and talk to her.[13]

When Lee arrived at the Lippincott offices she was admittedly very nervous. Lee mostly listened as Hohoff and her editorial team discussed what kinds of revisions would need to be done. At the end of the meeting, Lee agreed to do her best and went off to work on the revisions.

A short time later, Lee sent in her rewrite. While

Gregory Peck would play Atticus Finch in the film of Lee's novel. He poses here with his two young costars, Phillip Alford and Mary Badham.

there was still more work to be done, Lippincott decided to offer a contract. As Hohoff described the second draft:

It was better. It wasn't *right.* Obviously, a keen and witty and even wise mind had been at work; but was the mind that of a professional novelist? There were dangling threads of plot, there was a lack of unity—a beginning, a middle, an end that was inherent in the beginning. It is an indication of how seriously we were impressed by the author that we signed a contract at that point.[14]

When the novel was finally published in 1960, it was clear that Lee's hard work had paid off. Within the first year of publication, the novel sold more than half a million copies in ten languages. By 1961, it was awarded the prestigious Pulitzer prize. The film rights were also bought by a major Hollywood studio and a film version, starring Gregory Peck, got underway. Critics, however, were not as enamored with *To Kill a Mockingbird*. Several reviewers felt the child's narrative voice was unbelievable, while others thought the novel too sentimental.

Lee was overwhelmed by the publicity and the attention she was suddenly receiving. In an interview with Roy Newquist, Lee described her reaction to the novel's success:

> It was one of sheer numbness. It was like being hit over the head and knocked cold. You see, I never expected any sort of success with *Mockingbird*. I didn't expect the book to sell in the first place. I was hoping for a quick and merciful death at the hands of reviewers, but at the same time I sort of hoped that maybe someone would like it enough to give me encouragement. Public encouragement. I hoped for a little, as I said, but I got rather a whole lot, and in some ways this was just about as frightening as the quick, merciful death I'd expected.[15]

While the literary world was ready to make Lee a major celebrity, she shied away from all the attention. Lee became increasingly reclusive and protective of her privacy, refusing almost all interviews and public appearances. Journalist Kathy Kemp wrote, "For the rare reporter able to get her to offer up anything more than a stony look, she revealed, essentially, three things: her fondness for golf, her admiration for her father ('He is one of the few men I've known who has genuine humanity') and her plan to publish more and better novels." [16]

After the publication of *To Kill a Mockingbird*, Lee returned to Monroeville, where she worked on her next book. The writing process was enjoyable but difficult for Lee. She wanted to take her time to craft a work as good as her first novel. The next novel, however, never came to fruition. In fact, aside from three short magazine articles written in the early 1960s, she published nothing at all.

Working with Truman

Lee may not have produced another book of her own, but she was influential in helping an old friend with his newest work. In 1959, a murder case in Kansas caught the attention of Truman Capote. By then, Capote was a well-established author. Unlike the publicity-shy Lee, Capote loved the spotlight and was a famously flamboyant character

Harper Lee helped her childhood friend Truman Capote (pictured) with the research for his groundbreaking novel, In Cold Blood.

in the New York publishing world. He had been very successful with fiction and now wanted to try something new. In the process, he invented a whole new genre of literature, known today as true crime. After reading an article about the murder of the Clutters, a rural Kansas family, Capote decided to use the story as the basis of his new work. He would research the work like a journalist but present the story with the rich, descriptive narrative voice of a novelist. He invited his childhood friend to go with him to Kansas to help research the case.

According to Capote, Lee was enormously helpful with his research. In a 1966 interview, he said:

> I went with a lifelong friend, Harper Lee. She is a gifted woman, courageous, and with a warmth that instantly kindles most people. . . .
>
> She kept me company. . . . She went on a number of interviews; she typed her own notes, and I had these and could refer to them. She was extremely helpful in the beginning, when we weren't making much headway with the town's people, by making friends with wives of the people I wanted to meet.[17]

Lee and Capote became very involved with nearly all the major players of the case. They dined at the head detective's house the night the suspects, two drifters, were arrested. Later, in 1963, Capote and Lee attended the execution of one of the killers after he was found guilty and sentenced to death. The product of their labor was Capote's groundbreaking *In Cold Blood*, published in 1965. The dedication in the book read, "For Jack Dunphy and Harper Lee, with my love and gratitude."[18]

Retreating from the Limelight

Since her research trips with Capote, Lee has received many honors. In 1966, President Lyndon Johnson appointed her to the National Council of the Arts. She has been awarded several honorary degrees from prestigious schools, such as the University of Alabama and Mount Holyoke. Lee has attended some of the ceremonies, but always on the condition that she will neither speak nor grant interviews. Reporter Drew Jubera, who tried to track her down, wrote that Lee "vanished from the literary landscape, becoming nearly as enigmatic as Boo Radley."[19]

Lee, who never married, now divides her time between bustling New York City and the small Alabama town where she grew up. In Monroeville, she lives with her older sister Alice, a respected attorney like their father. The childhood home where they lived is now gone, replaced by Mel's Dairy Cream. The oak tree that inspired the hiding place for Boo Radley's gifts has long since been cut down. The famous courthouse, however, which was re-created to the smallest detail for the film, has been preserved as a historical landmark.

People in Monroeville see Lee around their small town, visiting shops or lunching every Sunday at David's Catfish Cabin with her sister. They let her go about her business, although she is often still asked for autographs. Most people in town know better, however, than to ask about her famous novel or her future publishing plans. Of course, many people still wonder why such a talented writer would choose never to publish another novel. As *To Kill a Mockingbird* only continues to gain in popularity and to speak to new generations of readers, however, some critics have begun to suggest that such speculation may be unfair. In the words of reporter Rheta Grimsley Johnson, Lee "authored an American classic, and that's good enough. . . . How many Pulitzer-winning, perennial best-sellers does a body have to write to satisfy the hordes, anyway?"[20]

CHAPTER TWO

Historical Background of the Novel

arper Lee's childhood was not the only real-life
inspiration for *To Kill a Mockingbird*—many historical events and societal attitudes also serve as important elements to the story. For example, the severe economic
hardships and deep-seated racial segregation that character-
ized the 1930s, the years during which Lee grew up, are
prominent features of the novel. While Lee's novel is set in
the 1930s, the themes of discrimination and tolerance also
resonated strongly within the social climate of the 1950s and
1960s, when the book was respectively written and published.
Critics argue that the atmosphere of the civil rights movement
affected both the composition and reception of the novel. Of
course, Lee's refusal to comment publicly on her novel makes
it difficult to confirm her intentions or influences. Even so, *To
Kill a Mockingbird*'s continued popularity supports the theory that the novel speaks to readers about issues that have
remained important well beyond the 1930s.

The Great Depression
In the 1930s, the United States was in the midst of the Great
Depression—the most severe and longest-lasting economic
slump the country has ever known. The depression began

when the stock market crashed in October 1929. The crash and the ensuing depression affected people from all walks of life. Industries of all kinds—from banks to small businesses to farms—lost massive amounts of money or went bankrupt altogether. The Southern states were particularly hard hit when the entire cotton industry, the region's major economic staple, went bankrupt.

Harper Lee alludes to particular hardships felt by the farming industry through her portrayal of the Cunningham family. This poor but respectable farming family lacks the money to buy basic necessities, such as food. Atticus Finch explains their plight further when he tells his son, "The Cunninghams are country folks, farmers, and the crash hit them hardest."[21]

One of the most significant indicators of the Great Depression was the unemployment rate. By 1932, an

The South was hit hard by the Great Depression. Poor Southern families lived in shanties like these.

unprecedented 25 to 30 percent of the workforce was unemployed. In cities across the country, regardless of size or geography, people stood in breadlines in hopes of receiving food to keep themselves and their families from starving. Even people with jobs were making significantly less than they had in the 1920s. Again, the situation in the South was much worse. The annual income in 1929 in the Southern states was $372 compared to $797 elsewhere in the country. Later, in 1935, the Works Progress Administration (WPA) was created under President Franklin D. Roosevelt to help the unemployed. The purpose of the program was to provide useful work for millions of victims of the Great Depression and, thus, to preserve their skills and self-respect.

Even with federal assistance, the unemployment rate led to fierce job competition. Across the country, it was common to see men and women hopping freight trains in hopes of finding jobs, food, and a better way of life elsewhere. In the South, where racial tension had always been high, the ill will between white and black people only intensified as everyone competed for the same handful of jobs. Many poor white men resented having to compete with black people for jobs they felt were rightfully theirs, and they blamed African Americans for their situations.

The intensified hatred that some white Southerners focused on African Americans is at the heart of *To Kill a Mockingbird*'s plot. Bob Ewell, the uneducated, unemployed father of Maycomb's poorest family, represents such bigotry at its worst. Unable, or unwilling, to provide for his family, Ewell lives with his children in a shack on the outskirts of town, next to the dump and near the black settlements. Ewell resents the black citizens of Maycomb and blames them for his condition. In a warped plan for revenge, he accuses an innocent black man of raping his daughter Mayella. Ewell hopes to destroy the lives of the people he feels have ruined his own. Despite the resentment he feels toward black people, however, Ewell is in reality a hate-filled, abusive alcoholic who does little to better himself or his situation. As Scout tells the reader, "He was the only man I ever heard of who was fired from the WPA for laziness."²² Even though his own laziness costs him his job, he still angrily blames others for his problems.

Racial Segregation

While all white Southerners may not have been as openly racist as Bob Ewell, they did participate in a system that blatantly denied African Americans many rights. As a means of upholding their power and dominance, white Southerners enacted laws that enforced racial segregation. Collectively, these laws were known as Jim Crow laws, named after a black minstrel show. The first segregation laws appeared after the Civil War and continued through the 1950s. While the particulars of Jim Crow laws changed from state to state, they invariably extended into all aspects of everyday life. Public buildings had separate entrances, drinking fountains, and bathrooms. Blacks and whites were not allowed to sit in the same sections of restaurants or on public buses. White people were granted exclusive access to facilities, such as parks, motels, and swimming pools. If a black person and a white person rode together in a car, one had to sit in the front, the other in back.

Throughout *To Kill a Mockingbird*, Lee adds scenes that depict Jim Crow in action. The courtroom, for example, which is supposed to be the seat of justice and equality, has separate seating areas for black and white people. When Jem and Scout are invited to sit in the "Colored balcony," four black men rise to give up their seats. Their gesture is not so much one of respect as requirement—by law, black people were obligated to give up their seats to any white person who wanted them. In addition to having separate schools and hospitals, black people were also expected to have their own

Segregation laws in the South prohibited African Americans from using drinking fountains designated for whites.

churches, as seen when Calpurnia, the Finches' housekeeper, takes the children to her congregation. Interestingly, in this scene, Lee includes an example of reverse discrimination when a woman from Calpurnia's church is upset to see white children there. She tells Cal, "You ain't got no business bringin' white chillun here—they got their church, we got our'n."[23] Jim Crow laws entrenched racial segregation so deeply that many citizens—both white and black alike—often accepted them without protest.

Other Jim Crow laws discouraged African Americans from voting. Peacoloa Barge, a black woman who grew up in Alabama in the 1930s, remembers:

Well, of course, we weren't allowed to register to vote. Even though I was a schoolteacher for twenty years, I didn't register to vote until the late sixties. There were a few black attorneys who would take on cases, but at least in Birmingham [Alabama] in the thirties and forties, black attorneys couldn't practice in the courthouse. Their very presence in the courtroom was bitterly resented by many people.[24]

Jury lists were derived from voter registration, so black citizens were not only kept from voting, but from serving on juries. By restricting African Americans' right to vote and denying them proper access to the legal system, the white population was able to maintain conditions as they were.

As demoralizing as the Jim Crow laws were, some white Southerners enforced segregation through intimidation and outright violence. Since the end of the Civil War, a secret organization of white men, known as the Ku Klux Klan, made it their mission to promote white Protestant supremacy through any means necessary. Membership in the Klan was at its highest during the 1920s, then dropped during the 1930s and 1940s.

Blacks were not allowed to serve on juries; nor could they sit with white spectators, as this courtroom scene from To Kill a Mockingbird *shows.*

Even without an organized group, racist whites took it upon themselves to terrorize nonwhites. Black people, mostly men, lived in fear of white lynch mobs that unlawfully judged and punished them. Lee captures the danger of such lynch mobs in one of the most dramatic scenes in the novel. The night before his trial, a mob approaches the city jail where Tom Robinson, the accused black man, is being held. They are so intent on harming Tom that they are willing to hurt their white neighbor, Atticus Finch, who is standing guard that night. One of the members of the mob even throws Atticus's twelve-year-old son Jem to the ground. While the fictional mob is eventually dispersed, real-life lynch mobs often caused much more serious harm. Lynching resulted in the violent, senseless murders of countless African Americans. According to historian Virginia Hamilton, in Alabama alone, between 1889 and 1940, there were 303 documented lynchings, almost all of which were against blacks.

The Scottsboro Trials

The racial tension between black and white people set the stage for one of the most infamous court cases of the day. The Scottsboro trials, as they are known, received enormous media attention. Later, they also served as one of Lee's inspirations for the fictional case against Tom Robinson, as evidenced by the many parallels between the cases.

In 1931, two white women accused nine black men of rape. The women, the black men, and a group of white men had all hopped aboard a freight train headed from Tennessee to Alabama. Along the way, the two groups of men began fighting. Although it was unclear who started the fight, the white men were thrown off the train in the course of the brawl. When the train arrived in Alabama, all the remaining riders were arrested on charges of vagrancy. One of the women, Victoria Price, was a known prostitute and the other was suspected of prostitution. In order to deflect attention

National Guardsmen escort the Scottsboro suspects to court. Harper Lee drew on this famous 1931 rape case as inspiration for her novel.

from their own illegal acts, the two women accused the nine black men of rape. Even though the police knew the prostitutes were not very reputable, they took their accusations seriously and arrested the nine men.

Similarly, the trial in *To Kill a Mockingbird* revolves around a white woman falsely accusing a black man of rape. Like Victoria Price, Mayella Ewell is not a respected member of society. Nonetheless, her charges are taken seriously simply because she is white and the accused is black. Also like Victoria, Mayella cries rape to detract attention from another crime—the physical and emotional abuse of her father.

Unlike the fictional case, which takes several months to come to trial, the "Scottsboro boys," as they were called, were brought quickly to court. Only twelve days after the initial arrest, the nine men were brought to trial. According to scholar Claudia Durst Johnson:

The chief witnesses included the two women accusers, one white man who had remained on the train and corroborated their accusations, another acquaintance of the women who refused to corroborate their accusations, the physician who examined the women, and the accused nine black men. The accused claimed that they had not even been in the same car with the women, and the defense attorneys also argued that one of the accused was blind and another too sickly to walk unassisted and thus could not have committed such a violent crime.[25]

In the court case Lee creates, the defendant, Tom Robinson, is also physically unable to have committed the crime of which he is accused. Even so, he is found guilty. Likewise, despite the lack of evidence in the Scottsboro trials, all nine black men were found guilty after a three-day trial. Eight of the nine were sentenced to death.

The Scottsboro case went through several rounds of appeals until it was finally heard before the U.S. Supreme Court. The Court ordered new trials for all nine defendants on the basis that they had not received adequate legal representation.

The second round of trials began in March 1933. This time around, the proceedings took longer. The defense called more witnesses, including a doctor who testified he saw no sign of forced intercourse during his medical examination of the plaintiffs. One of the two women recanted her testimony altogether, admitting she and her friend Victoria had made up the rape charges. Still, the all-white jury found the defendants guilty and once again sentenced them to death.

During the second round of trials, the presiding judge, James Horton, shocked the community with an unprecedented legal decision. Not believing there was enough evidence for a guilty verdict, let alone a death sentence, Judge

Horton overturned the jury's conviction. In an eloquent statement, Horton condemned not only Victoria Price for making false accusations, but also the jury for finding the black men guilty on the basis of such faulty evidence.

Horton's relentless belief in justice is mirrored in the novel through the character of Atticus Finch. Despite the pressure from his community, Atticus, like Horton, stands up for the rights of African Americans. Atticus also shares the same firm belief in the ideals for which the legal system is supposed to stand. Horton emphasized these ideals in his address to the jury in the Scottsboro case: "So far as the law is concerned, it knows neither native or alien, Jew or Gentile, black or white. This case is not different from any other. We have only our duty to do without fear or favor."[26]

In the novel, Atticus's final argument touches on many of the same themes. His emphasis on justice and the duty of the jurors to uphold it is remarkably similar to Horton's remarks.

> But there is one way in this country in which all men are created equal—there is one human institution that makes a pauper the equal of a Rockefeller, the stupid man the equal of an Einstein, and the ignorant man the equal of any college president. That institution, gentlemen, is a court. . . . A court is only as sound as its jury, and a jury is only as sound as the men who make it up. I am confident that you gentlemen will review without passion the evidence you have heard, come to a decision, and restore this defendant to his family. In the name of God, do your duty.[27]

Sadly, the greatest similarity between the two trials may be the fact that both the real and fictional juries ignore the plea for a fair verdict. Tom Robinson is found guilty and sentenced to death. In the Scottsboro case, although Horton reversed the decision, retrials and appeals went on for several years, while the nine black men remained in prison. Finally, in

1935, two of the convictions were reversed by the U.S. Supreme Court on the grounds that African Americans had been deliberately excluded from possible jury pools. Eventually, some of the defendants were paroled. One man, much like Tom Robinson, was shot by a deputy in an attempted jailbreak. The last of the falsely accused defendants was not released until 1950.

The Civil Rights Movement

Also possibly influencing Lee were the events of the civil rights movement unfolding around her at the time she was writing. During the 1950s, the civil rights movement blossomed, partly as a result of two major events that occurred in Alabama and took place within four years of the publication of *To Kill a Mockingbird*. Although the reclusive author has never confirmed their influence, scholars such as Claudia Durst Johnson argue that it is "doubtless . . . that the events of those years in which the work was conceived had a decided effect on the novel itself."[28]

The first major rallying point for the civil rights movement was the simple but defiant gesture of a black woman refusing to give up her seat on a bus. When Rosa Parks would not offer her bus seat to a white patron in Montgomery, Alabama, on December 1, 1955, the result was a yearlong bus boycott and a major revival in the black community's concentrated efforts to overturn segregation laws. The next year, in 1956, a young black woman named Autherine Lucy applied and was admitted to the University of Alabama. When she arrived on campus, however, protests broke out in response to allowing a black student on campus. The events in Alabama received national attention and set off a series of counterprotests across the country.

Parks's and Lucy's struggles were only two in a series of movements to end segregation. In 1957, schools in Little Rock, Arkansas, were ordered to be desegregated.

Some scholars believe that the events of the civil rights movement influenced Harper Lee's work. Protests such as this march on Washington, D.C., were a hallmark of the movement.

(Segregation was actually ruled unconstitutional in 1954 in the famous *Brown* v. *Board of Education* case, but many schools were slow to implement desegregation.) Protests were so violent that federal troops were called in to enforce the court-ordered desegregation. In 1960, the year *To Kill a Mockingbird* was published, students in Greensboro, North Carolina, organized a sit-in as an attempt to integrate restaurants and diners. Throughout the 1960s, nonviolent protests, as well as some violent attacks, took place across the country.

Lee grew up during the height of segregation and wrote while the major battles over these laws were being fought. On one hand, Lee's novel depicts the events of a different time. On the other, she uses the obviously unfair trial of Tom Robinson to comment on the injustices that continued to exist in her own day. In doing so, Lee "criticizes the morality of 1930s *and* 1960s America" [emphasis added],[29] according to critic Carolyn Jones. Lee's novel points to the many ways that conditions had not changed at all during the years between the 1930s and 1950s. The same Jim Crow laws that kept the fictional courtroom segregated in *To Kill a Mockingbird*, for example, continued to keep Rosa Parks from sitting where she wanted on a public bus in 1955. While the momentous events of the 1950s civil rights movement may not have made their way directly into the pages of *To Kill a Mockingbird*, the central issues of social justice and tolerance that they illuminated can certainly be found throughout.

The Public Response and Censorship Debates

The public response to *To Kill a Mockingbird*—both positive and negative—further demonstrates the ways in which the novel spoke to contemporary issues. While critical reviews of the novel were mixed, the public response was overwhelmingly positive. In only one year, the novel sold over five hundred thousand copies and was awarded the Pulitzer prize for fiction. The book not only sold vast quantities, but it also provided readers profound insight into the ways they looked at major social issues. In a 1992 interview, for example, James Carville, President Clinton's campaign manager and a lifelong Southerner, remembered entirely rethinking his attitude toward African Americans after first reading the novel in the 1960s. "I just knew, the minute I read it, that she [Lee] was right and I had been wrong."[30] The novel also resonated with high school teachers, who began using the novel in the 1960s to introduce their students to issues of discrimination and tolerance.

As *To Kill a Mockingbird* was introduced to more and more classes, however, it began receiving negative attention from some parents and citizens who felt the subject matter was inappropriate for students. By the mid-1960s, schools and libraries were banning the novel from their shelves, arguing it was immoral. The objections raised ranged from questionable language to references to sex and violence to negative depictions of authority figures. Critic Jill P. May argues that the real underlying reason for many of the objections, particularly those from conservative Southerners, could also be the "candid portrayal of Southern white attitudes." [31] In other words, May argues that some white Southerners did not appreciate the way they were depicted in the novel and hoped that by labeling it immoral, fewer readers would have access to it.

The most public of the censorship debates took place in Richmond, Virginia, where, in 1966, the book was banned from libraries and school reading lists. Over the course of several months, a heated debate took place in the pages of the local newspaper, the *Richmond News-Leader*. Those against the censorship efforts often made note of the novel's value in teaching students lessons relevant to their own day and time as an argument to overturn the ban. As one editorialist wrote, the novel is a "sensitive, frightening, awakening, truthful presentatio[n] of what could happen and what is happening in our life today. Why hide truth from our young people? We need to teach them right and wrong." [32]

The last word in the *News-Leader* debate was given to Lee herself, who wrote in to defend her novel. The idea that *To Kill a Mockingbird* was somehow immoral was completely perplexing to her. In an editorial response she wrote, "Surely it is plain to the simplest intelligence that 'To Kill a Mockingbird' spells out in words of seldom more than two syllables a code of honor and conduct . . . that is the heritage of all Southerners." [33]

Beginning in the 1980s, the protests against *To Kill a Mockingbird* shifted in nature, when some African American citizens began criticizing its inclusion on their children's reading lists. Some parents felt that regardless of all else, at

Gregory Peck and Harper Lee on the film set of To Kill a Mockingbird.
Even today, Lee's novel remains a subject of controversy.

the end of the story, an obviously innocent black man is found guilty and, thus, the novel represents, and even reinforces, institutionalized racism. As late as 2002, black parents in Novia Scotia were calling for the removal of the novel from their children's classrooms on the basis that it contained racial slurs. According to the American Library Association, the novel has ranked as one of the one hundred most frequently challenged books every decade since its publication, including 1990 to 2000.

Continued Appeal

Despite the censorship debates, the novel's popularity has never died down. In fact, in 2003, *USA Today* listed *To Kill a Mockingbird* as one of the top 150 best-selling books of the year. The novel also remains a perennial staple in high school English classrooms, offering new generations of students insight into the powerful social themes that were important in the 1930s, critical in the 1950s and 1960s, and that will remain important for years to come.

CHAPTER THREE

The Plot

T o *Kill a Mockingbird* is a story about growing up in the Southern United States in the 1930s. It is told from the point of view of an adult woman looking back at herself as a six- to eight-year-old child. On one hand, Scout Finch, the narrator and protagonist, tells the story of a typical childhood—of summer games with her brother Jem and friend Dill, of first experiences in school, and of life in a small town. At the same time, Scout's childhood is extraordinary in many ways: She learns to read and write before entering school; she is raised by a single father, whom she calls by his first name; and she lives in a town with fascinating and eccentric people.

In the same way, the story that Scout relays is also a mixture of unique and universal elements. The first half of the story revolves mostly around the Finches' neighbor Boo Radley and the children's attempts to get him to come out of his house. The details of Scout's adventures, the emphasis on their setting in the Deep South, and

Scout and her father Atticus Finch share a quiet moment on their porch.

the distinctive character of Boo Radley are all unique elements to her story. The trial plot, which makes up the second half of the story, is directly influenced by the particular time and place of the novel. Even so, the lessons Scout learns are still broad enough for the story to have relevance in any time period.

Chapter 1

The book begins with Scout remembering the summer her brother Jem broke his arm. As she narrates, she reveals some of her family's history, including the fact that the Finches have been living in Alabama for generations. Scout's father Atticus, a well-respected lawyer, chose to raise his family in the small town of Maycomb.

Although Maycomb and the South are in the midst of the Great Depression, Atticus manages to make a comfortable living. He, Jem, and Scout live in a house on the town's main street. Their housekeeper and cook, an old black woman named Calpurnia, is at the house most days as well. Scout's mother died when she was only two, so she has few memories of her.

During the summer when Scout is almost six and Jem nearly ten, an odd boy named Charles Baker Harris comes to stay with Rachel Haverford, the Finches' neighbor. The boy, who goes by the nickname Dill, is seven, but is very small for his age. The three quickly become friends, playing together nearly every day that summer. Their favorite activity is trying to make Boo Radley come out of his house.

Boo Radley, whose real first name is Arthur, lives in the run-down Radley place, but no one has seen him come out for years. As a young man, Boo got in trouble with the police for a juvenile stunt. As punishment, his father, and later his brother Nathan, have locked him in the house ever since. Dill, in particular, is fascinated with the mysterious stories he hears of Boo and becomes obsessed with making him come out. He dares Jem to touch the Radley house, which Jem grudgingly agrees to do. Scout is convinced that she sees a shutter move as Jem runs away from the house.

Chapter 2

As summer ends, Dill returns to his home in Mississippi and Scout eagerly awaits the first day of school. Once she gets to class, though, she is sorely disappointed. Her teacher, Miss Caroline, is a stranger to Maycomb's ways and deals poorly with children. When Miss Caroline discovers that Scout can already read and write, she gets very upset and tells Scout to stop immediately. Scout is annoyed at her teacher for making her believe her knowledge is a crime.

That afternoon, Miss Caroline unknowingly offends Scout's classmate, Walter Cunningham Jr., by offering to lend him a quarter for his lunch. She does not realize that Walter will not be able to repay her. Thinking she is helping, Scout explains, "You're shamin' him Miss Caroline. Walter hasn't got a quarter at home to bring you."[34] Embarrassed by her own ignorance, Miss Caroline punishes Scout, smacking her on the hand with a ruler.

Chapter 3

Before lunch that day, Scout tries to beat up Walter for getting her in trouble. Jem stops her and instead invites Walter to their house to eat. At the table, Scout makes fun of Walter for putting too much syrup on his food. This time it is Calpurnia who reprimands Scout, telling her she must always be polite to guests no matter who they are.

Back at school, Miss Caroline is mortified to learn that a student, Burris Ewell, has lice. When she tries to send him home to get cleaned up, he laughs rudely. He tells her, "You ain't sendin' me home, missus. I was on the verge of leavin'—I done done my time for this year."[35] As Miss Caroline soon learns, the Ewells, Maycomb's poorest family, only come to class on the first day of school as a gesture to make town officials happy.

Later that night, Scout tells Atticus of her awful day and complains about Miss Caroline. Atticus suggests she consider how Miss Caroline feels before reaching a snap judgment. Atticus tells his daughter, "If you learn a simple trick, Scout, you'll get along better with all kinds of folks. You never really understand a person until you consider things from his point of view . . . until you climb into his skin and walk around in it." [36] Scout agrees to try to heed Atticus's advice but still says she does not want to go back to school. She argues that if Burris Ewell does not have to, neither should she. Atticus explains that, in her case, the law demands she go to school. As a compromise, he promises to continue reading with her, as long as she does not tell her teacher.

Chapter 4

The school year continues slowly for Scout, who is bored by her classes. Walking home from school one day, Scout discovers a stick of gum hidden in a knothole in one of the Radley's oak trees. Later, she and Jem find two Indian-head pennies in the same spot.

Summer returns at last and so does Dill. To pass the summer days, the children begin acting out stories about Boo Radley. Atticus catches them and asks if they are making fun of the Radleys. Jem lies and says no. Scout insists they should stop playing, but Jem teases her until she changes her mind.

Chapter 5

As summer wears on, Jem and Dill begin to spend more and more time together without Scout. She is left to spend time with her neighbor Miss Maudie Atkinson. Miss Maudie tells Scout more about Boo's life. She explains that he is really the victim of an extremely harsh father and had always been a nice, polite young man. She also says, however, that if he was not crazy as a child, he probably is by now.

The next morning, Scout joins Jem and Dill and is pleased when they do not chase her away. They have decided to entice Boo out by writing him a nice note. Now that she knows more about the reclusive man, Scout tries to discourage the boys. They do not listen. Atticus catches them and demands that they stop harassing Boo.

Chapter 6

On Dill's last day in Maycomb, the children disobey Atticus and sneak over to the Radley property to peer in his windows.

Scout, her brother Jem (left), and Dill (John Megna) plot to draw the reclusive Boo Radley out of his house.

Jem and Scout examine two soap figures they have found in the Radley's oak tree.

Scout warns them against their plan, but in the end decides to join when Jem insults her pride by saying she is acting more like a girl. As they tiptoe to the window, someone inside sees the children and fires a shotgun. Terrified, the children run away. Jem gets stuck on a fence and must take off his pants to escape.

The neighbors gather after hearing the shot. Miss Stephanie Crawford, the town gossip, tells everyone that Nathan Radley was shooting at a Negro in his yard. Dill comes up with an elaborate story about why Jem is missing his pants. Atticus believes the fib, but tells Jem he must go get his pants. Scout is terrified for her brother to return to the Radley house. Jem is also scared, but he is determined to go in order to avoid admitting that he lied to Atticus.

Chapter 7

School begins and Scout is once again disappointed. At least this year, she and Jem can walk home together. One afternoon, Jem tells his sister that the night he went back for his pants, he found that they had been mysteriously mended and folded. He says it was "like somebody was readin' my mind . . . like somebody could tell what I was gonna do." [37]

As time passes, Scout and Jem find more treasures in the oak tree, including two carved soap figures, a medal, and a pocket watch. They decide to leave a thank you note. On their way to deliver it, they discover the hole has been filled with cement. The next day they run into Nathan Radley, who claims he sealed the hole because the tree is dying. As Jem points out to Scout, the tree is completely healthy.

Chapter 8

For the first time in years, it snows in Maycomb. Jem and Scout want to make a snowman, but there is not enough snow. Instead, they make a figure out of dirt and cover it with snow. That same night, there is a fire at Miss Maudie's house. All the neighbors come to help put it out. In the confusion, someone drapes a blanket over Scout's shoulders. Jem realizes it is Boo. He tells Atticus and also explains to him about the gifts left in the tree.

Chapter 9

As Christmas draws near, Scout nearly gets in a fight at school when Cecil Jacobs, a boy from Scout's class, makes fun of her father. He tells the other children that "Scout Finch's daddy defend[s] niggers."[38] Scout does not know what he means, but she beats him up anyway.

At home, she tells her father about Cecil Jacobs's remarks. Atticus explains that he will be defending a black man named Tom Robinson, who is accused of raping a white woman. He tells Scout, "You might hear some ugly talk about it at school, but do one thing for me if you will: you just hold your head high and keep those fists down."[39] Scout promises to try. The next day, when Cecil taunts Scout again, she remembers her promise and walks away from a fight for the first time in her life.

Three weeks later, the Finches go to Aunt Alexandra's, Atticus's sister, for Christmas. Scout does not get along well with her aunt because she tries to force her to act more "lady-like." Despite her promise to her father, Scout attacks her whiny cousin Francis when he calls Atticus a "Nigger lover."[40] Her Uncle Jack punishes her. Scout later complains to him that he did not listen to her side of the story first. When he hears why she attacked Francis in the first place, he apologizes but still tells her fighting is not an answer. Later that night, Scout overhears her father and Jack talking about the case and how Tom Robinson is innocent but doomed to be judged guilty.

Chapter 10

After Christmas, Scout and Jem are eager to learn how to shoot the air rifles their father gave them as gifts. Their father will not teach them to shoot, however, because, according to Uncle Jack, Atticus does not have an interest in guns. Uncle Jack teaches them instead.

Scout and Jem take Atticus's refusal to show them how to shoot as a sign of weakness. They are disappointed that Atticus is older than their friends' fathers. They assume his age keeps him from doing "normal" fatherly activities, such as hunting, fishing, and smoking. Their opinion of their father changes dramatically, though, when a mad dog named Tim Johnson appears in the street. Not only is Atticus the only one who can stop the dog, he is able to shoot him dead with just one shot.

Chapter 11

As the year continues, Atticus spends more time at his office preparing for the trial. From time to time, the children walk to town to visit him. In order to get to his office in Maycomb's business district, they pass the home of Mrs. Dubose, a cranky old woman who always shouts nasty comments at them. Atticus warns his children to just ignore her. After a particularly harsh remark about Atticus, though, Jem forgets his father's warning and tears up her flowerbed in retaliation. As punishment, he is forced to go to her house every day to read to her. Scout accompanies him, even though it means

Believing their father has no interest in guns, Scout and Jem are amazed when Atticus kills a mad dog with a single shot.

listening to Mrs. Dubose yell at them for a little longer each day. After a month she dies. Atticus reveals to Jem that she was addicted to morphine and that the reading was part of her effort to combat her addiction.

Chapter 12

Jem begins to hit puberty and becomes increasingly distant from Scout. Scout also learns that Dill will not be coming to visit that summer, leaving her with no playmates. Atticus is forced to travel to the state legislature for the upcoming trial, leaving the children with Calpurnia. Calpurnia takes the children to mass at her all-black congregation. The children are treated with great respect because they are Atticus's children. They listen as Reverend Sykes asks the congregation to help a man named Tom Robinson and his family. Scout realizes that Tom is the man her father is defending and asks Calpurnia for more details about the crime.

Chapter 13

The children return from church to find Aunt Alexandra has moved in to their home. Much to Scout's chagrin, Aunt Alexandra immediately insists her niece act more like a girl and take greater pride in the Finch family history. She even convinces Atticus to scold his children about their behavior. He does, but later apologizes for his lecture, telling Scout she should forget his words.

Chapter 14

Although Atticus stops lecturing the children about the Finch family, they hear plenty about the subject from townspeople and classmates. Scout and Jem are teased increasingly for Atticus's role in Tom Robinson's trial. Scout asks for a better explanation of what the trial is about. During the conversation, the trip to Calpurnia's church is mentioned. Aunt Alexandra is mortified that the children went to a black congregation and insists they never return. She also tries to convince Atticus to fire Calpurnia, telling him the housekeeper is no longer necessary now that she's staying with the family. Atticus flatly refuses.

Later that night, Scout and Jem find Dill hiding in their bedroom. He has run away from home. Jem informs Atticus and he calls Dill's mother to get permission for him to stay for the summer.

Chapter 15

A week after Dill's arrival, a group of men led by Sheriff Heck Tate come to Atticus's house in the evening. Sheriff Tate explains that Tom Robinson is being moved to the Maycomb jail and that there might be trouble from the local white men as a result. A few days later, Atticus receives a phone call and goes to guard the jailhouse where Tom is being kept. The children follow him and watch as a lynch mob approaches the jail. Not realizing the danger, Scout runs out to greet her father. Atticus insists Jem take them home, but the boy, in his first act of manhood, refuses.

Scout notices that one of the members of the mob is Walter Cunningham's father, Walter Cunningham Sr. She tells him that she's in Walter's class and innocently asks him to say hi to Walter. Mr. Cunningham is suddenly embarrassed by what he is about to do. He tells Scout he'll pass her regards to his son and then convinces the rest of the group to go home. Unintentionally, Scout had managed to disperse the mob. Atticus is very proud of both his children, although anxious to get them home.

Chapter 16

The morning the trial is set to begin, Atticus discusses the danger of mob mentality with his children. He explains that even good people, such as Mr. Cunningham, can be convinced

Atticus faces a mob that has come to the jail to lynch Tom Robinson. Atticus's children have followed him and witness the confrontation.

to do bad things. Given the previous night's danger, he asks that they not go near the courthouse during the trial. The children sneak in to the trial anyway, which is packed with people. Scout overhears some men talking and learns for the first time that her father never chose to defend Tom Robinson, but rather was appointed counsel by Judge Taylor. As she ponders this new information, she and Jem look for a seat but cannot find one. Reverend Sykes, the minister from Cal's church, notices and invites them up to the "Colored balcony." Several black men give up their seats for Scout, Jem, and Dill.

Chapter 17

The trial gets under way with Judge Taylor presiding. Sheriff Heck Tate and Bob Ewell, Mayella's father, are called as witnesses. During cross-examination, Sheriff Tate admits to Atticus that a doctor was never called to examine Mayella Ewell, the woman alleging rape. Atticus also gets Heck to reveal that a left-handed person would have more likely beaten Mayella. During his cross-examination of Bob Ewell, Atticus points out to the jury that he is left-handed.

Chapter 18

The next witness to testify is Mayella Ewell. Although Atticus knows she is lying about what happened, he still treats her with respect. Unaccustomed to such kindness, Mayella assumes he is making fun of her. Atticus pleads with Mayella to admit that there was no rape and that her father beat her, but she does not. As they listen to Mayella's version of the story, Jem and Scout notice that Tom Robinson's left arm is crippled and useless. They realize he could not have committed the crime as it is being described.

Chapter 19

The prosecution rests and Atticus calls Tom, his only witness. During his testimony, Tom explains that he had been to the

Atticus questions Tom Robinson (Brock Peters) in court. Although Robinson's testimony is compelling, the white spectators are not impressed.

Ewell home on several occasions at Mayella's request to help her with various household chores. On the night in question, he reveals to the jury that she attempted to seduce him. Tom's testimony is powerful, but his case goes badly when he admits to the prosecutor on cross-examination that he initially agreed to help Mayella because he felt pity for her. The white crowd is unsettled because they do not like Tom's answer. Dill gets very upset with the way the prosecutor is treating Tom and the lies the Ewells have been telling. When he starts crying, Scout takes him outside.

Chapter 20

As the children leave the courthouse, they meet Dolphus Raymond, a white man who lives with his black mistress and their biracial children. Rumor has it that Raymond is the town drunk. They discover, however, that Raymond only pretends to be drunk so as not to have to answer questions about his choice of lifestyle. After talking with Raymond, Scout and Dill return to the courthouse just in time to hear Atticus's powerful closing argument.

Chapter 21

As Atticus finishes, Cal approaches to tell him that his children are missing. Mr. Underwood, the newspaper editor, had noticed the children in the balcony much earlier and informs Atticus of their whereabouts. Atticus is upset to learn his children have been in the courthouse the whole time. Even so, he agrees to allow them to stay to hear the verdict. Jem is confident that they have won. A few hours later, the jury returns with a guilty verdict. Jem is devastated. The courtroom empties, and as Atticus goes out, Reverend Sykes makes the children rise with the rest of the people in the "Colored balcony" as a gesture of respect for their father.

Atticus comforts Jem, who is distressed over the guilty verdict.

Chapter 22

Jem is extremely upset by the verdict. The children spend time with Miss Maudie, who tries to shelter them from the town gossips. She is not wholly successful—Miss Stephanie Crawford comes over to tell them that Bob Ewell has threatened Atticus for embarrassing him at the trial.

Chapter 23

Everyone but Atticus is nervous about Bob Ewell's threats. He uses their concerns as an opportunity to discuss the trial and its larger implications about racism and prejudice. He admits that a legal system that can convict an innocent man simply because he is black is blatantly unjust. He also says, however, that the amount of time it took the jurors to deliberate gives him hope that changes to that system might be coming in the future. He reveals that the single juror who initially wanted to acquit Tom was none other than Mr. Cunningham.

Hearing this, Scout asks if she can invite Walter over to play. Aunt Alexandra adamantly tells Scout no because she feels that women in their family should not like people like the Cunninghams. Scout and Jem discuss this hypocrisy, but cannot come up with an easy answer to why people unfairly judge those who are different. Jem wonders if such prejudice is the reason why Boo Radley chooses to stay inside and away from society.

Chapter 24

Toward the end of the summer, Aunt Alexandra invites Scout to tea with the ladies from the Missionary Society. Scout helps serve tea and tries to participate in the ladies' conversation. She is upset, however, that the neighborhood ladies cannot recognize their own prejudices and hypocrisy. While they lament the condition of Africans, they do not see the oppression of black Americans in their own town. Atticus interrupts the party to tell Cal that Tom Robinson has been killed in an attempted escape from jail. As Atticus leaves with Cal to break the news to Tom's family, Scout resolutely determines to go back to the party and do her best to act the part of a lady.

Chapter 25

Before he leaves for the summer, Dill tells Scout about what happened when Atticus went to tell Helen Robinson of her husband Tom's death. As Atticus and Cal were driving to the Robinsons' house, they came across Dill and Jem, who were coming home from the swimming hole. They agreed to give them a ride, but said they needed to stop at the Robinsons' first. Dill describes the black settlements to Scout and also says that Helen collapsed when she was told her husband had been killed.

News of Tom's death occupies the town. Mr. Underwood, the openly racist editor of the town newspaper, writes an editorial saying that Tom's death was the murder of an innocent man. The other big reaction comes from Bob Ewell, who ominously says that Tom's death was only one of three deaths he'd like to see happen.

Chapter 26

School begins again. The children are no longer afraid of Boo, but still hope he will come out. Third grade is as unpleasant for Scout as the rest of her formal education has been. Her teacher, Miss Gates, praises the ideals of democracy and criticizes the persecution of the Jews in Europe. Scout also remembers hearing Miss Gates make racist remarks about African Americans during the trial. When she asks Jem about this hypocrisy, he gets upset and tells her never to mention the trial again. Later, Atticus explains that Jem is still having a hard time accepting the outcome of the trial.

Chapter 27

By the middle of October, life in Maycomb returns to normal, with the exception of three events. First, Bob Ewell acquires, then loses a job with the Works Progress Administration (WPA) in a matter of days. He irrationally blames Atticus for his downfall and promises to get revenge. Then, there is a break-in at Judge Taylor's house. Although no one can prove it, everyone suspects it was Ewell trying to get revenge on the judge for making him look foolish during the trial. Finally, Ewell begins harassing Helen Robinson, Tom's widow. Link Deas, Helen and Tom's employer, threatens to have Ewell arrested if he continues.

In the meantime, the school is having a Halloween party. Scout is in a pageant where each child dresses up as a food produced in the state. Scout dresses up in a ham costume, which impedes her ability to move and see, so Jem must lead her to the school. On the way, Cecil Jacobs scares them by jumping out from behind a tree. At the school, the pageant goes smoothly until Scout misses her cue to go on stage. Jem tells her not to worry about her mistake and leads her home.

Chapter 28

On the way home from the pageant, the children realize they are being followed. At first, they think it is Cecil again, but Jem soon senses they are in danger. Jem tells Scout to run just as they are attacked. Scout cannot see because of her costume, but she hears her brother scream and runs in that direction. She runs into someone, who begins crushing her inside her costume. Suddenly, a fourth person pulls the attacker off her. She calls for Jem, but hears only heavy breathing in response. She struggles out of her costume in time to see a stranger carrying Jem's limp body to her house.

Chapter 29

The Finches call for a doctor, who declares Jem has only a broken arm. The sheriff arrives and informs Atticus that Bob Ewell has been stabbed to death. Scout tells everyone what happened. As she gets to the part about a stranger helping them, she realizes her savior is in the room. She turns to him and says simply, "Hey, Boo."[41]

Chapter 30

Scout takes Boo onto the porch. Boo never says a word. They listen to Heck and Atticus argue about what to do. Atticus says Jem acted in self-defense, but Heck corrects him, saying Ewell fell on his own knife. Atticus refuses to allow his son's actions to be covered up. Heck adamantly sticks by his version of the story, finally explaining that it was Boo who killed Ewell. Atticus realizes it might indeed be better to pretend the killing was an accident than to force the recluse into the

The mysterious Boo Radley (Robert Duvall) murders Bob Ewell, the man who attacked Jem and Scout.

limelight. Scout reassures her father that they made the right decision. The child tells her father that exposing Boo Radley would "be sort of like shootin' a mockingbird." [42] Atticus is pleased with Scout's reply. Then he turns to Boo and thanks him for saving the children.

Chapter 31

Scout asks Boo if he would like to see Jem before he goes home. When Boo silently nods yes, Scout takes him upstairs to say good night to Jem. She then walks him home, taking care to slip her hand in the crook of his arm. She wants to make sure that anyone who might be watching them realizes that Boo is like any other gentleman. Boo gets to his house without ever having said a word to Scout. She never sees him again, but is happy knowing that, for just a moment, she was able to imagine the world from his perspective. She returns home and finds Atticus sitting in Jem's room. He reads one of Jem's books to her in her room until she falls asleep, then returns to Jem's room to spend the night so he can be there the next morning when his son wakes up.

CHAPTER FOUR

The Cast of Characters

For many readers, the characters of *To Kill a Mockingbird* are the most memorable aspect of the novel. Scout, the willful tomboy; Atticus, the moral lawyer; and especially Boo Radley, the eccentric neighbor, have all become classic characters in American literature. More important, it is through such characters that many of the novel's greatest lessons are taught.

Aunt Alexandra

Aunt Alexandra is Atticus's sister, who comes to stay with the Finches once the trial gets under way. She is strong willed and fiercely proud of her family's heritage. She often criticizes Atticus and his children for not living up to the Finch family name.

Being rooted in such tradition and history, Aunt Alexandra also adheres to the old-fashioned social codes of the South. She tries always, for example, to play the part of a "proper" Southern woman—dressing in feminine clothes, associating only with people of a high social class, and not discussing taboo subjects. She firmly believes that people's class, gender, and race set them within a certain place in society, and she frowns upon any interaction between social sets. As Scout says:

> Aunt Alexandra was one of the last of her kind: she had river-boat, boarding school manners; let any moral

come along and she would uphold it; she was born in the objective case; she was an incurable gossip. . . . She was never bored, and given the slightest change she would exercise her royal prerogative: she would arrange, advise, caution, and warn.[43]

Aunt Alexandra's obsession with tradition and propriety often leads to conflicts of will with her independent, spirited niece. She tries tirelessly to get Scout to wear dresses instead of overalls and to play with toys that other young girls play with. She is so concerned with turning Scout into a cookie-cutter image of what she believes a young girl should be that she cannot see Scout for the unique individual she already is.

Miss Maudie Atkinson
Maudie Atkinson is the Finches' quick-witted, sharp-tongued neighbor across the street. Next to Atticus, she is one of Maycomb's most open-minded citizens and is always quick to publicly stand up for what she believes in. She is proud to be one of the few people in town who believes in equality for whites and blacks. Miss Maudie often talks to the children, particularly Scout, while tending her beloved garden. She helps Scout better understand Atticus's actions, Boo Radley's history, and life in a small town. Like Atticus, she respects and teaches Scout to reach her own conclusions, rather than lecturing her like other adults often do.

In contrast to Aunt Alexandra, Miss Maudie also serves as a positive female role model for Scout. As Scout describes, "She was a widow, a chameleon lady who worked in her flower beds in an old straw hat and men's coveralls, but after her five o'clock bath she would appear on the porch and reign over the street in magisterial beauty."[44] The image of Miss Maudie as both an androgynous gardener and a majestic queen of the porch suggests that a more fluid, less rigid definition of womanhood is possible.

Calpurnia

Calpurnia is the Finches' black housekeeper and cook. Although she is a stern disciplinarian, she is a faithful member of the Finch family and the closest thing to a mother Scout has ever known. Cal is one of the few black members of the community who can read and write. She even teaches Scout to write before she begins school, mostly as a means to keep Scout from bothering her on

Calpurnia (Estelle Evans), the motherly housekeeper, is a treasured member of the Finch family.

rainy days. Cal also serves as Jem and Scout's connection between the white world of Maycomb and the black community.

Miss Stephanie Crawford

Stephanie Crawford is the town gossip. She constantly starts unfounded rumors within the town. She even takes pleasure in being the first to tell Scout and Jem that Bob Ewell has threatened their father.

Walter Cunningham Jr.

Walter Cunningham Jr. is one of Scout's classmates. Although his farming family is poor, they are hardworking, honest, and proud. At school, when Walter is unable to pay for lunch and is too embarrassed to say why, Scout explains to the teacher on his behalf. After she gets in trouble as a result, she tries to beat him up in the school yard. Walter later comes to the Finches to eat and, much to Scout's surprise, chats like an adult with Atticus about life on the farm. He tells Atticus that he's still in first grade because he gets behind when he misses school to help his father with the farm in the spring. Through Walter, Scout begins to understand that a person can still be decent and good, even if he or she is lower on the social hierarchy.

Walter Cunningham Sr.

Walter Cunningham Sr. is the father of Scout's classmate Walter. He is a poor but honest and hardworking farmer. After Atticus provides him with some legal services, Mr. Cunningham pays in produce because he has no cash. He continues delivering goods to Atticus until his debt is paid in full.

Mr. Cunningham is also a member of the mob that threatens Atticus and Tom Robinson at the jailhouse. He serves as an example of how an otherwise good person can get caught up in mob mentality. Mr. Cunningham comes back to his senses, however, when Scout singles him out of the mob to speak to him. She reminds him of his individual humanity and, as a result, he stops to think about his actions and ultimately disperses the mob. Later, he is the only juror to consider acquitting Tom Robinson of rape.

Link Deas

Link Deas is Tom and Helen Robinson's employer. He takes it upon himself to speak up on Tom's behalf at the trial. While his intentions are good, he is thrown out of the court-house for disrupting the proceedings. After the trial, he makes certain Helen is not harassed by Bob Ewell as she passes his house on her way to work.

Mrs. Henry Lafayette Dubose

Mrs. Henry Lafayette Dubose is a crotchety old woman who lives in the Finches' neighborhood. In order to get to town, Scout and Jem must walk by her house and endure the racist comments she yells at them. When Jem can no longer take her abuse, he pulls up her flowers in retaliation. As punishment, Atticus makes him read to her every day for a month, during which she continues to spew vicious insults. She dies shortly after the sessions are done. Atticus reveals that the old woman was actually a morphine addict and that the reading was part of her effort to fight her addiction. Although he does not agree with her opinions, Atticus admires Mrs. Dubose's courage in battling her addiction. He tells his children, "She was the bravest person I ever knew."[45] In that way, Mrs. Dubose forces the children to reevaluate their definition of what it means to be brave.

Bob Ewell

Bob Ewell is the uneducated, unemployed father of the Ewell clan, the poorest family in Maycomb. Ewell is a drunk who physically and sexually abuses his daughter Mayella, the woman accusing Tom Robinson of rape. Ewell recognizes that he is the lowest of the low in Maycomb's white social hierarchy. To make up for his own lack of status, Ewell is all too happy to go along with Mayella's accusation against a black man—a man belonging to the one group of people below even him on the social ladder.

In the end, however, Ewell's warped plan for revenge backfires. Although Tom Robinson is found guilty, everyone in town knows Ewell and his daughter were lying. Atticus has also exposed Ewell as a terrible, abusive father and has shown Mayella had come on to Tom. By accusing Tom Robinson, Ewell only furthers his reputation as an ignorant, racist, hate-filled man. Later, he not only rejoices in Tom's death, but also attempts to redeem himself by harming innocent children. Ewell is meant to represent the forces of pure, inexplicable evil and ignorance that exist in the world.

Mayella Ewell

Mayella Ewell is the lonely, abused, nineteen-year-old woman who accuses Tom Robinson of raping her. She is born into a terrible position in life and has little hope of ever escaping it. She remains uneducated because she is forced to watch her brothers and sisters all day while their drunken father is away. When he returns, she must endure his abuse day after day. Her dreams for a better life are symbolically represented by the geraniums she lovingly grows in her otherwise dismal home.

Like her father, Mayella realizes that one of her few opportunities for power in society is to abuse a black man. By seducing Tom, Mayella knows she will have control over another human being for the first time in her miserable life. Ironically, while she craves respect and compassion from men, she has no idea how to respond when she finally receives it. When Atticus questions her courteously during the trial, she assumes he is making fun of her and refuses to cooperate.

Although Atticus questions Mayella with sensitivity, the ignorant young woman is uncooperative, believing that he is mocking her.

Atticus Finch

Atticus Finch is the widower father of Scout and Jem and is a prominent, well-respected lawyer in Maycomb. He has a strong sense of right and wrong and is arguably Maycomb's most open-minded, tolerant citizen. As a result, he serves as the novel's moral compass and the voice of reason.

Unlike other citizens of Maycomb, Atticus does not succumb to strict, hypocritical social mores. He does not raise his children according to standard societal rules, but rather as openly and honestly as possible. While he provides them with the guidance that all children need, he also treats them as adults, even allowing them to call him by his first name. When Scout asks loaded questions, such as, "Do you defend niggers, Atticus?"[46] he not only gives her a lengthy explanation, but also calmly explains why she should not use racial slurs.

Atticus's unique style of parenting also encourages his children to consider things from other people's perspective. Rather than allow Scout to simply complain about Miss Caroline, he suggests she think about how she would feel as a new teacher in an unknown community. Atticus also pushes his children to reach beyond the face value of a situation to understand the whole truth. According to Scout, "Do you really think so . . . was Atticus's most dangerous question."[47] This question forces his children to think deeper before reaching an easy conclusion.

Interestingly, Atticus employs this same respectful line of questioning with adults. During the trial, he speaks with the same courtesy and respect whether questioning Sheriff Tate, Mayella Ewell, or Tom Robinson. He is able to maintain his basic respect and faith in people regardless of gender, class, or race, because he can accept both their good and bad qualities. While he cannot condone Mayella's lying on the stand, he still recognizes the hardships of her miserable, young life.

Although idealistic, Atticus recognizes that even a superb defense cannot save his innocent client.

Atticus also believes strongly in the law he defends and the ideals of the legal system he represents. He is sincere when he tells the jury during his closing argument that the court is the "one human institution that makes a pauper the equal of a Rockefeller, the stupid man the equal of an Einstein, and the ignorant man the equal of any college president."[48] Even so, Atticus also realizes that in a prejudiced society his case is doomed to fail before it gets under way. The fact that he still mounts the best defense he can offers hope for the ideals of justice and tolerance that he strives to uphold.

Jean Louise "Scout" Finch

Scout Finch is the narrator and young protagonist. Over the course of the story, she ages from six to eight. Being so young and innocent, Scout is able to report on the complicated events of the story with honesty and objectivity. At the same time, though, it is important to note that the story is actually being told by an adult Jean Louise as she looks back on the events as perceived by her childhood self. While Scout's childhood voice prevails in the novel, the two points of view sometimes overlap. For example, when Scout is caught eavesdropping on a conversation between Atticus and Uncle Jack, she wonders how her father knew she was listening. The adult narrator, however, reveals to the reader that she now knows her father wanted her to hear his conversation. "It was not until many years later that I realized he wanted me to hear every word he said." While the young Scout represents childish curiosity, the adult Jean Louise represents an element of wisdom that comes with age.

Scout is an exceptional young girl for the time and age in which she lives. She is extremely intelligent, learning to read and write before stepping foot in a classroom. She is also a tomboy, preferring overalls to dresses, climbing trees to tea parties, and beating up her classmates to calm, rational discussions. In many ways, Scout becomes the individual she is because of the unique parenting style of her father Atticus. Rather than enforcing social norms by which most residents of Maycomb live, Atticus grants his daughter the freedom and respect to make her own choices. At times, this freedom leads toward childish errors in judgment—such as her unfair perception of Boo Radley as a monstrous freak. More often than not, though, Scout is more honest, open-minded, and moral than most of the adults in her community.

Scout's intense curiosity allows many important questions to be raised. At the beginning of the story, these questions are the product of childish imagination. She wants to know who Boo Radley is and how she might make him come out. As she matures, she considers more complicated questions, such as *why* he might choose to stay inside.

As Scout grows up, she must also face the fact that evil exists in the world she once believed to be simply good and safe. The unjust trial of Tom Robinson, in particular, forces Scout to see the world in a more realistic light. One of the central themes of the novel is whether having to confront evil will destroy Scout, as it has Boo and Tom, or whether she will rise above it to become a just, moral adult like her father.

In the end, Scout is indeed able to hold on to her basic faith in the world. She internalizes Atticus's most important lesson—that one must consider things from other people's points of view. By the end of the novel, she is no longer afraid of Boo, but rather sees him as a good man who has been hurt by a cruel world. As critic Carolyn Jones writes of this final episode:

> Scout learns Atticus's ethic completely. Looking at her life from Boo's perspective, she is able to see herself and her experiences in a new way. This is the imaginative "Do you really think so?" and is the birth of Scout the writer and is the education of Scout as a moral agent. She also makes an act of compassion—and this is her gift, as the neighbor, to Boo: she sees the world from his point of view and gains an understanding of him that no one else in Maycomb has ever had and, since he enters his house never to emerge again, ever will have.[49]

By seeing things from Boo's perspective, Scout demonstrates that she will follow her father's example and grow into the kind of moral, just adult who can hold onto her faith, even in the face of cruelty and intolerance.

Jeremy Atticus "Jem" Finch

Jem Finch is Scout's older brother, who ages from ten to thirteen over the course of the story. As Jem grows from a boy to a young adolescent, he more literally represents the transition from childhood to adulthood. At the beginning of the novel, he is Scout's playmate, climbing trees alongside her and teasing her mercilessly at times. By the novel's end, however, Jem has assumed the role of protective older brother, walking her to and from her school pageant and doing his best to save her from Bob Ewell's attack.

As Jem becomes a young man, he is forced to reevaluate many of his childhood perspectives. Ten-year-old Jem, for example, defines the concept of bravery as accepting Dill's dare to touch the Radley house. Jem is scared to go near the house, so he assumes accepting the dare will prove his bravery. Over the course of the novel, his interactions with other people broaden that simple definition. From Mrs. Dubose, he learns that bravery can mean overcoming a personal obstacle. From his father, he learns that a truly brave man stands up for his beliefs and morals despite the consequences. Atticus's example makes Jem want to grow up to be a fair and just lawyer, too.

The process of accepting an adult worldview is not always an easy one for

Jem is traumatized by the events surrounding the trial.

Jem. During the trial, Jem is confident that justice will prevail and is nearly shattered when a guilty verdict is returned. Scholar Claudia Durst Johnson argues that "Jem, in particular, is traumatized because the law in theory had been sacred to him, but in practice it is mendacious [false], uncovering a powerful, concealed code at work in complete contradiction to written law."[50]

At first, it is unclear whether Jem will recover from the shock or whether he will succumb to the same fate as Boo and Tom. Atticus tells Scout not to worry,

> that Jem was trying real hard to forget something, but what he was really doing was storing it away for a

while, until enough time passed. Then he would be able to think about it and sort things out. When he was able to think about it, Jem would be himself again.[51]

Indeed, by the end of the novel, things do settle down. One night after the trial, Jem tells his sister not to crush a bug she finds in their room. When she asks why, he explains that they "don't bother you" and, therefore, shouldn't be harmed. Through his protection of a vulnerable, innocent creature, it is suggested Jem will be able to slowly but surely regain his faith in humanity and will grow into a decent man like his father.

Uncle Jack Finch

Uncle Jack is Atticus and Alexandra's bachelor brother. Atticus is ten years his senior and worked to put him through medical school. Jack now practices medicine outside Maycomb, although he returns for one week each year at Christmas. Jack is adored by his niece, even though he suggests she act more ladylike and not curse or fight. When he later catches her fighting with her cousin Francis, he punishes her for not heeding his advice. Scout is more upset that her uncle did not listen to her side of the story than the fact that she had been punished. After he and Scout discuss how he could have better handled the situation, Jack admits to his own brother that he has a lot to learn about raising children.

Miss Caroline Fisher

Miss Caroline Fisher is Scout's first-grade teacher. She is well meaning and well intentioned, but not well versed in the ways of life in Maycomb. She supports John Dewey's approach to education, which advocates learning by doing. Yet when she discovers Scout can already read and write, she does not encourage her to continue, but rather commands she stop altogether. It is because of inadequate teachers like Miss Caroline that Scout finds she learns less in the classroom than she does through simple life experience.

Miss Gates

Miss Gates is Scout's third-grade teacher. After a student brings in a newspaper article on Hitler, Miss Gates informs her class about the atrocities being committed against the Jews in Europe. She also takes the opportunity to contrast the German and U.S. governments. According to Scout: "Then Miss Gates said, 'That's the difference between America and Germany. We are a democracy and Germany is a dictatorship. Dictator-ship,' she said. 'Over here we don't believe in persecuting anybody. Persecution comes from people who are prejudiced. Prejudice,' she enunciated carefully." [52]

Despite her lesson, however, Scout finds Miss Gates confusing. After the trial, Scout had overheard Miss Gates making racist comments about African Americans. The hypocrisy makes no sense to Scout, who wonders, "how you can hate Hitler so bad an' then turn around and be ugly about folks right at home." [53]

Charles Baker "Dill" Harris

Dill Harris is the nephew of one of the Finches' neighbors, who comes from Meridian, Mississippi, almost every summer to stay with his aunt. Short for his age, Dill is an imaginative, fun boy who quickly becomes friends with Jem and Scout. Dill, in particular, is fascinated by Boo Radley and is the first to come up with the idea of making him come out of his house.

Dill's wild imagination also leads him to come up with some tall tales. He often concocts elaborate lies, much to Scout's frustration. Many times, his lies keep him from having to admit hard truths, including that he does not know his biological father or that his mother and stepfather are not as kind toward him as they could be. Ironically, despite his penchant for lying, it is Dill who becomes distraught in the courthouse after listening to the Ewells make up stories on the stand.

Dill is also an outsider to life in Maycomb. He comes to understand it through his own observations and through what he learns from Scout and Jem. In that way, he mirrors the role of the reader, who must also come to the novel as an "outsider" and objectively listen to the story.

Miss Rachel Haverford

Rachel Haverford is the Finches' neighbor and Dill's aunt. Miss Haverford lets her nephew stay with her in Maycomb almost every summer.

Dill's role is that of the outsider, who observes the novel's events from an objective perspective.

Arthur "Boo" Radley

Boo Radley is the Finches' mysterious, reclusive neighbor who becomes the object of the children's obsessive imaginations. Despite being unfairly perceived as a freakish oddity, Boo cares deeply for the children, leaving them small gifts, taking care of them when they least expect it, and ultimately saving their lives when they are attacked.

As a young man, Arthur got in minor trouble with the police and was unfairly punished the rest of his life by his cruel father. As a result of being locked away from society, Arthur is no longer able to function as a normal member of the community. He serves as one of the novel's two symbolic mockingbirds in that he is a good person whose life has been destroyed by forces outside his control.

Nathan Radley

Nathan Radley is Arthur's older brother, who takes over the role of Arthur's "keeper" after their father dies. Like their father, Nathan unfairly keeps Arthur secluded from the rest of society. He even cuts off one of Boo's few connections with the outside world when he seals over the knothole in the tree in which Boo leaves gifts for Scout and Jem.

Dolphus Raymond

Dolphus Raymond is a wealthy white businessman who lives on the outskirts of town with his black mistress and their biracial children. The townspeople believe Dolphus is a drunk, which they consider is the only possible explanation for his behavior. Scout and Dill discover, however, that the drunkenness is really just an act. As Dolphus explains:

> I try to give 'em a reason, you see. It helps folks if they can latch onto a reason. When I come to town, which is seldom, if I weave a little and drink out of this sack, folks can say Dolphus Raymond's in the clutches of whiskey—that's why he won't change his ways. He can't himself, that's why he lives the way he does.[54]

Just as Dill becomes sick after listening to the Ewells' false testimony, Dolphus has become jaded by witnessing a lifetime of white people's hypocrisy and as a result has chosen not to live among them.

Tom Robinson

Tom Robinson is the black man Atticus defends against an unjust accusation of raping a white woman. Tom is a kind, hardworking sharecropper whose left arm is crippled. It is the color of his skin, however, that is his greatest physical obstacle. While he literally dies during an attempted jailbreak, his

The racist prejudices of the courtroom make Tom Robinson's innocence irrelevant.

life is figuratively over the moment Mayella Ewell falsely cries rape.

Tom is the only witness Atticus calls for the defense, and it is through his honest testimony that the reader learns what happened the night Mayella alleges she was raped. When Mayella asked Tom to help her move some furniture, Tom was willing to help, but when she began to seduce him he protested. Once he realized that Bob Ewell had witnessed Mayella come on to him, Tom knew he was in an impossible situation—if he stayed, he would be in almost as much trouble as if he ran. In other words, Tom recognized his precarious position as a black man in a society controlled by white people. For the same reason, Tom decides to take his chances by breaking out of jail rather than face another all-white jury in his appeal. Like Boo Radley, Tom becomes a symbolic mockingbird once evil prejudice and societal forces destroy this innocent, vulnerable man.

Reverend Sykes

Reverend Sykes is the pastor of the black congregation in Maycomb. He is one of the linchpins of the black community, practically demanding his congregation support Tom

Robinson and his family through their ordeal. It is from Reverend Sykes that the children learn just how much it means to the black community that their father is defending Tom Robinson. He finds them seats in the "Colored balcony" of the courthouse when there is no other place left to sit. Even after the case has been lost, he makes them rise as a gesture of respect when their father passes by.

Heck Tate

Heck Tate is Maycomb's sheriff. He is a decent man who tries to uphold the law as fairly as possible. When an unruly lynch mob threatens to take the law into its own hands and murder Tom Robinson, Sheriff Tate warns Atticus of the danger. In court, Heck is called as a witness for the prosecution, but his honesty on the stand makes him more of an asset to Atticus's defense. He admits never having called a doctor on the night Mayella was allegedly raped. He also provides testimony that makes Atticus realize a left-handed person must have beaten Mayella.

While Heck Tate represents the law at its best—tolerant, color-blind, and just—he is ironically the one to suggest lying about Bob Ewell's death. In order to save Boo Radley, Heck adamantly sticks to the false story of Ewell falling on his own knife. He explains to Atticus, "To my way of thinkin', Mr. Finch, taking the one man who's done you and this town a great service an' draggin' him with his shy ways into the limelight—to me, that's a sin. If it was any other man it'd be different. But not this man, Mr. Finch."[55] Although the resolution has fallen outside the bounds of the law, Tate believes justice is best served by not letting others know of Boo Radley's involvement in Ewell's death.

Judge John Taylor

Judge John Taylor is the judge at Tom Robinson's trial. He appoints Atticus to defend Tom instead of Maxwell Green, the usual court-appointed defense attorney. According to Miss Maudie Atkinson, Judge Taylor had Tom's best interest in mind when he assigned Atticus to the case. As Miss Maudie says, although Judge Taylor knows Atticus cannot win the case, he realizes that the moral-minded lawyer would offer the best defense possible. After the trial, there is an attempted burglary at Judge Taylor's house. Everyone suspects Ewell was trying to seek revenge on Judge Taylor for making him look foolish during the trial.

Braxton Braggs Underwood

Braxton Braggs Underwood is the owner, editor, and printer of the *Maycomb Tribune*, the town newspaper. He lives and works in an office building across from the jailhouse, in the center of town. Although he openly despises black people, Underwood defends Tom Robinson's right to a fair trial. When a lynch mob threatens to murder Tom Robinson at the jailhouse before the trial even begins, Underwood is prepared to defend him. As Atticus and his children leave to go home, Underwood reveals that he had been watching with a loaded shotgun in order to protect them from danger.

After the trial, when Tom Robinson is killed during an attempted jailbreak, Underwood provides the most moving eulogy in town. He writes an eloquent editorial in which he compares Tom's death to the killing of innocent songbirds. For an openly racist man to condemn Tom's killing underlines the injustice that has occurred.

CHAPTER FIVE

Literary Criticism

The 1950s, during which *To Kill a Mockingbird* was written, and the 1930s, the years during which it was set, were both periods of especially turbulent race relations between blacks and whites in the United States. Tensions were particularly high in the Southern states. It seems natural, then, that so much of Lee's novel focuses on racial prejudice and inequality. Scenes of blacks and whites attending separate churches or sitting in different designated sections of the courthouse clearly illustrate segregation at work. Likewise, the unfair trial of Tom Robinson, which makes up the second part of the novel, shows that society has very different rules for its black and white citizens. By depicting everyday injustices, Lee's novel joins other major American works that comment on racial inequality, such as Mark Twain's *The Adventures of Huckleberry Finn* and Harriet Beecher Stowe's *Uncle Tom's Cabin*.

Of course, race is not the only theme Lee explores. Critic Edgar Schuster believes that the "achievement of Harper Lee is not that she has written another novel about race prejudice, but rather that she has placed it as an aspect of a larger thing."[56] In other words, Lee may write about racial prejudice, but more as a means of highlighting the complicated issues that are a part of all human relationships. Part of the novel's enduring appeal is the way in which it opens discussion of powerful, universal themes such as justice, courage, evil, and compassion.

Lee writes of this "larger thing" without ever lecturing the reader. While the story is told from the eyes of the adult Scout, she is looking back at the events as perceived by her childhood self. Important life lessons and experiences are allowed to unfold naturally for the reader. By presenting complicated issues through the eyes of a child, Lee does not need to preach about what is wrong and what is right, but rather allows the reader to draw his or her own conclusions.

Social Codes and Prejudices

As in any society, the citizens of Maycomb group and judge one another by a number of superficial categories. Race, gen-

Racial prejudice in the 1950s forced African Americans to ride at the backs of buses.

der, and class are only a few of the factors that shape relationships in the novel. As certain groups are granted more power or respect than others, a hierarchy, or ranking system, emerges. In terms of class, for example, the Finches and other educated, white townspeople are most respected. They hold the positions of greatest power in the town, such as sheriff, judge, and teacher. Poorer, working-class farmers, such as the Cunninghams, are considered beneath the townspeople. Although they have less social status, these country folk are still respected members of the community because they are hard-working and honest. The Ewells, however, who are abusive and lazy, are below the farmers. According to Scout, the Ewells "had been the disgrace of Maycomb for three generations." [57] At the very bottom of the social ladder are the black members of society. Although they may be more honorable and admirable than the Ewells, their skin color alone determines their place in society.

Because power is never distributed equally, the lower members of the hierarchy are often subjugated to the higher members. For example, this unfair power structure is what allows the Ewells to get away with falsely accusing Tom Robinson of a crime he did not commit. The Ewells know they are the lowest of the low among Maycomb's white citizens. With no education, no jobs, and no social status, the only leverage they have is the fact that they are white. Claudia Durst Johnson, one of the few scholars to devote considerable attention to Lee, argues: "Having no whites to look down upon, those whites who live in poverty vent their rage against black men and women." [58] In other words, one of the few ways that Bob Ewell can make up for his own lack of importance in society is to persecute the only social group lower than himself.

Mayella Ewell is also denied any position in society, not only because of her class status, but because of her gender as well. She has little choice but to take her father's abuse day after day. Ironically, like her father, one of the few opportunities she has to be in a rare position of power is to victimize a black man. Her true motivation for seducing Tom Robinson is revealed during his testimony. Tom tells the jury, "She reached up an' kissed me 'side of th' face. She says she never kissed a grown man before an' she might as well kiss a nigger. She says what her papa do to her don't count." [59] Seducing Tom is a maneuver for power as much as for attention. She has the power to control his fate whether he accepts or rejects her advances. Mayella cannot fight back against her own father, nor does her social status offer the chance to interact with more respectable men. She chooses instead to manipulate the same system that has been abusing her for years.

It is not only the Ewells who show Maycomb's social hierarchy at its worst. Lee also critiques the social system, and the prejudice that can result from it, through her depictions of higher-status citizens, such as Aunt Alexandra. Alexandra presumes herself superior to nearly all of Maycomb's inhabitants. Aunt Alexandra will not allow Scout to play with the lower-class Walter Cunningham, nor will she let her visit Calpurnia in the black part of town. She believes doing so would be beneath the Finches. Alexandra also has set ideas about gender. She always criticizes Scout for not being more ladylike.

For Alexandra, the superficial categories—like race, class, and gender—that divide society are exclusive. She believes that mixing among the neat, albeit artificial, groupings is improper. Alexandra's belief in such categories leads Scout to the conclusion that "Aunt Alexandra fitted into the world of Maycomb like a hand into a glove, but never into the world of Jem and me." [60]

The Mockingbird as Symbol

While Scout may find society's prejudices confusing and irritating, they are nonetheless powerful forces in Maycomb. So powerful, in fact, that some characters are destroyed completely when confronted with terrible injustice. Lee represents these characters through the symbol of the mockingbird. After giving Scout and Jem air rifles, Atticus tells his children, "Shoot all the bluejays you want, if you can hit 'em, but remember it's a sin to kill a mockingbird." [61] Miss Maudie further explains that mockingbirds do not do anything to harm anyone, but rather just make beautiful music. Thus, the phrase "to kill a mockingbird" means to destroy something that is utterly innocent and vulnerable.

The Finches are pictured with Calpurnia and their neighbor, Maudie, in a scene of racial harmony rare in Maycomb.

In the course of the novel, two characters in particular represent the metaphor of the title. The first is Tom Robinson, who is found guilty of a crime he did not commit simply because he is black. During the trial, Atticus offers evidence that Mayella was beaten by her father, not Tom. Even so, the all-white jury cannot take the word of a black man over that of a white man—doing so would disrupt the rigid social codes they live by, unjust as they may be. After Tom is shot while attempting to escape, Mr. Underwood, the editor of the town paper, compares his death to "the senseless slaughter of songbirds by hunters and children."[62] "Songbird" alludes to the title of the novel. The comparison of a harmless songbird to the vulnerable black man emphasizes the sadness of something good and innocent being overpowered by negative forces outside its control.

The other symbolic "mockingbird" of the novel is Boo Radley. Like Tom, whose skin color predetermines his social status, Boo Radley's place in society is fixed because of the family into which he was born. The Radleys' choice to keep to themselves has consequences for their son. From the beginning, he is seen as an outsider and is treated with as much prejudice as the town shows Tom Robinson. People imagine him as a monster, a criminal, and a freak without ever attempting to discover the truth.

Although Boo is not killed like Tom, he, too, symbolizes a slaughtered mockingbird. After committing a juvenile offense, Boo's overly strict parents keep him inside for most of his life. As a result of being locked away from society, he becomes unable to function fully as a normal member of the town. By the end of the novel, Scout comes to realize that the path of Boo's life has been largely outside his control. She understands that exposing Boo's crime to the rest of the town will only serve to destroy him further. She tells Atticus that turning him in would "be sort of like shootin' a mockingbird."[63] In other words, she recognizes that it would be cruel to bring additional suffering to a man who acted out of innocence and good intentions.

Coming-of-Age: From Innocence to Experience

It is only by the novel's end, however, that Scout learns to understand Boo's situation. In the beginning, she takes part in demonizing Boo by publicly enacting the events of his life and trying to get him to come out of his house. Her change of view takes place over the course of the novel while she grows from a six-year-old to a nine-year-old. As she matures, she learns more about herself and the world around her. In that way, the transition and the various paths one is presented with while moving from childhood to adulthood become central themes of the novel.

The childhood world Scout presents at the beginning of the novel is carefree and fun. She, Jem, and Dill play games of make-believe, swap comic books, and challenge each other with double dares. Scout believes without question in the safety of her world. When she finds gum in a tree, even a tree belonging to the eccentric Radleys, there is no debate as to whether she should eat it. "The gum looked fresh. I sniffed it and smelled it all right. I licked and I waited for a while. When I did not die I crammed it into my mouth." [64]

At first, Scout seldom questions the social order of her community. When classmate Walter Cunning-ham, one of the country folks,

Calpurnia's values lead Scout to question her own and also those of society.

comes to the Finches' for dinner, Scout feels perfectly justified in making fun of him for pouring too much syrup on his food. Scout is surprised when Calpurnia yells at her for her judgments. Calpurnia explains, "Don't matter who they are, anybody sets foot in this house's yo' company, and don't let me catch you remarkin' on their ways like you was so high and mighty!" [65] Although she does not want to do so, Scout is forced by Cal to rethink the way she blindly accepts society's strict mores.

Jem more literally represents the transition from a child-like point of view to a more adult one as he goes through puberty during the course of the story. As a ten-year-old, Jem defines bravery in terms of accepting Dill's dare to touch the Radley house. In Jem's mind, because he is scared to touch

81

the Radley house, running up and doing so will prove to Dill that he is brave. Through the course of the novel, that simple definition changes as Jem begins to recognize the courage of his father's actions. He realizes it takes a much braver person to stand up for what he or she believes in than to accept a simple dare. Courage is no longer a physical act for Jem, but rather a moral one.

Jem tests this new definition of courage when he refuses to obey Atticus for the first time. As a lynch mob surrounds Atticus, he tries to get his son to return home. Jem firmly tells Atticus that he will not leave. Unlike Scout, who does not fully grasp what is happening, Jem makes a conscious, adult decision to stand by his father and the ideals for which he is fighting.

As Scout and Jem make their way from a state of pure innocence to a more adult one, they are forced to ask difficult questions: "Atticus . . . what exactly is a nigger-lover?"[66] and "What's rape Cal?"[67] In other words, one of the largest

Jem's growing maturity is evident as he discusses the trial with townspeople.

challenges the children face is how to incorporate their new experiences with evil into an understanding of the world they believed to be fundamentally good and safe.

The novel's symbolic mockingbirds, Boo Radley and Tom Robinson, demonstrate that evil can be an overpowering force. As R.A. Dave writes, "Two such innocent victimizations paralleled with each other intensify the tragic view of the world and recall the terrifying prognosis: 'So shall the world go on: to good men malignant, to bad men benign.'" [68] Essentially, the "terrifying prognosis" is that bad things can inexplicably happen to good people, and bad people can go unpunished.

When the guilty verdict forces Jem to confront the harsh reality of racism, this injustice threatens to break him much the same as it did Boo and Tom. After hearing Atticus's final arguments, Jem proclaims definitively, "We've won it. . . . Don't see how any jury could convict on what we heard." [69] Jem's faith in justice, and even in humanity, is temporarily shattered when the guilty verdict comes in.

Perhaps what keeps Jem from being destroyed like Boo and Tom is the fact that Atticus serves as his moral guide. Unlike other characters in the book, Atticus understands that most people have both good and bad qualities. In order to make sense of these opposing forces, Atticus appreciates a person's good qualities, but tries also to understand the bad by considering things from another person's point of view. Atticus demonstrates this moral philosophy to his children several times. He forgives Mr. Cunningham, for example, for taking part in the lynch mob that threatens him. "Mr. Cunningham is basically a good man," he said. "He just has his blind spots along with the rest of us. . . . Mr. Cunningham was part of a mob last night, but he was still a man." [70]

Both Scout and Jem take Atticus's examples seriously as the novel unfolds and their characters mature. His lessons offer a more hopeful picture for the kinds of adults these children will become. Whereas Scout initially sees Boo Radley as a freakish oddity, she realizes by the end of the novel that he is a human being. In reality, Boo commits a violent crime to save the children, but for Scout the evil of his actions is outweighed by the good of his intentions. Her ability to see things from his perspective suggests she will continue to follow Atticus's example. She will not lose faith altogether as she progresses from innocence to experience.

The Education of Children

While Scout's open-mindedness suggests her moral education is a great success, the same cannot be said for her formal education. In fact, the moral education that Atticus provides his children is the near opposite of the education they receive in school. As Edgar Schuster writes:

> In the course of their growing up the children do a great deal of learning, but little of that learning takes place in school. Jem and Scout learn from experience; their teachers are not Miss Caroline and Miss Gates, but Atticus, Calpurnia, and Alexandra. Their most effective "teacher," however, is life itself, their experience.[71]

It is no coincidence that the majority of Scout's story takes place during the summers, when school is not in session. Doing so allows Lee to highlight the important learning that comes simply from life experience.

Ironically, learning through experience is the school's philosophy. What Jem mistakenly refers to as the "Dewey Decimal System" is actually an approach to early childhood education promoted by John Dewey. Dewey's approach supports learning by doing. Miss Caroline, however, becomes so obsessed with Dewey's theory that she fails to make it the actual practice in her day-to-day classroom work. When Miss Caroline catches Scout writing, she tells her to tell Atticus to "stop teaching her." "Besides," she says, "we don't write in the first grade, we print. You won't learn to write until you're in the third grade."[72] Rather than allowing Scout to continue "doing," Miss Caroline forces Scout to stop. As a result, Scout becomes less interested in school.

Even as a child, Scout recognizes the difference between an official and an unofficial education. Having no comparison by which to judge her school's teaching methods, Scout thinks to herself:

> I could only look around me: Atticus and my uncle, who went to school at home, knew everything—at least, what one didn't know the other did. . . . Jem, educated on a half-Decimal half-Duncecap basis, seemed to function effectively alone or in a group, but Jem was a poor example: no tutorial system devised by man could have stopped him from getting at books. As for me, I knew nothing except what I gathered from *Time* magazine and reading everything I could lay hands on at home, but as I inched sluggishly along the treadmill of the Maycomb County school system, I could not help receiving the impression that I was being cheated out of something.[73]

What Scout is being "cheated out of" in school is a certain quality of lessons learned. Scout and Jem not only learn more outside the classroom, but they learn more important lessons as well. As Schuster asks: "What can Miss Caroline teach about getting along with others when she herself knows virtually nothing about the human beings she is instructing? And what can Scout learn about democracy in action from Miss Gates, who worries about Negroes 'getting above themselves' and marrying whites?"[74]

The most important lessons of the novel—lessons of tolerance, courage, and morality—are ones Scout and Jem learn far outside the walls of the classroom. At the novel's end, it is

Scout learns far more under her father's guidance than she does at school.

again Scout, in her typically comical fashion, who recognizes how much more she has learned through her experiences during the summer than she had in school: "As I made my way home, I thought Jem and I would get grown but there wasn't much else for us to learn, except possibly algebra." [75]

Practice v. Preaching: Inequalities in the Legal System

Like the educational system, the legal system is represented as having two opposing sets of ideals: one which is professed and one which is actually practiced. Lee clearly places questions of law and legality at the center of her novel by casting a lawyer and his legal-minded children as the main characters, as well as by making Tom Robinson's trial the driving action of the plot. In addition, as Claudia Durst Johnson points out, the law permeates both the setting and the relationships among many of the characters:

The cement of Maycomb, a community whose "primary reason for existence was government" is shown to be its formal and informal law: entailments (to which poor but honest Mr. Cunningham falls victim), compromise (between Scout and Atticus over her reading, for example), state legislature bills (introduced by Atticus, a legislator), treaties (between the Finch children and Miss Maudie over her azaleas), truancy laws (that the poor and lawless Ewell children, but not Scout, are allowed to break), hunting and trapping laws (which are violated by Bob Ewell), and bending the law (an issue on which the novel closes). The pervasiveness of legal allusions even extend to Calpurnia, who has been taught to read, and teaches her son to read, using Blackstone's Commentaries.[75]

The law also serves to highlight once more the theme of injustice with social hierarchies. While Tom Robinson is legally entitled to a trial by his peers, no black men are allowed to sit on the jury. Much to Scout's frustration, women are also excluded from participating. Within the courthouse, the supposed seat of blind justice, black spectators are legally required to sit separately from the white citizens. The scene in which four black men rise to give Jem, Scout, and Reverend Sykes their front-row balcony seats may seem like a gesture of respect for the minister, or perhaps for Atticus, but in truth, the men would have been required by law to offer their seats to any white person who wanted them.

Atticus realizes that, within such a system, he is essentially defeated before even stepping foot in the courtroom. He admits to his brother Jack, "You know, I'd hoped to get through life without a case of this kind, but John Taylor pointed at me and said 'You're it.'"[77] However, in order to be able to stand up for his values and to be a good role model for his children, Atticus still mounts the best defense he can. As Carolyn Jones argues, Atticus still believes that "the legal system offers at least a *chance* of success. In contrast to the lynch mob in the dark, the court represents the light of reason."[78]

It is to this "chance" of what a trial can represent that Atticus appeals in his closing argument:

But there is one way in this country in which all men are created equal—there is one human institution that makes a pauper the equal of a Rockefeller, the stupid man the equal of an Einstein, and the ignorant man the equal of any college president. That institution, gentlemen, is a court. It can be the Supreme Court of the United States or the humblest J.P. court in the land, or this honorable court which you serve. Our courts have their faults, as does any human institution, but in this country our courts are the great levelers, and in our courts all men are created equal.[79]

Atticus and Tom stand as the guilty verdict is read. The novel highlights the injustice caused by racism.

The power of Atticus's closing argument and the integrity to which he appeals almost makes the verdict itself seem momentarily irrelevant. His case is a moral victory in the sense that it publicly praises tolerance above prejudice and justice above privilege.

Of course, that symbolic victory is of little consolation to Tom Robinson, who must deal with the deadly consequences of the legal loss. Tom's fate demonstrates that the idea that "all men are created equal" ultimately fails black men. Recognizing that the appeal process will yield no different results for him, Tom breaks out of jail. Eight-year-old Scout also demonstrates a profound understanding of the reality of the legal system when she thinks "Atticus had used every tool available to free men to save Tom Robinson, but in the secret courts of men's hearts Atticus had no case."[80] In the end, the superficial prejudices that the jury believes in contradict the official law.

Ironically, while Atticus supports the law of the land at all costs, it is the flawed, self-governed system of Maycomb that saves his children. Bob Ewell is the picture of everything illegal. He hunts off-season, he physically and sexually abuses his daughter Mayella, and he threatens Atticus and his family. Even so, he is never persecuted the way innocent Tom Robinson is. At most, Link Deas, the Robinsons' employer, merely threatens to have Bob Ewell put in jail for harassing Helen, Tom's widow. What eventually stops Ewell is not a legal, democratic process, but a violent, illegal crime. As Claudia Durst Johnson further argues:

> Even a humane and civilized system of law becomes at some point and under certain circumstances severely limited when primitive, hidden codes or lawlessness emerge so powerfully. In the case of Boo Radley's killing of Bob Ewell, law is proven inadequate for another reason—specifically, that on occasion laws and

Although Atticus champions the law, it is Boo Radley's violent crime, the murder of Bob Ewell, that saves Scout and Jem.

boundaries must be overridden for justice to be done.[81]

In this final scene, the morals Atticus promotes clash with the law he works to defend. Despite his reluctance, Atticus must acknowledge that the moral thing to do—namely let Boo go unpunished—is a more just decision than holding him responsible to the law.

Lee thus ends her novel by once again complicating traditionally opposed concepts—right and wrong, good and evil, and immoral and moral are never clear-cut categories in *To Kill a Mockingbird*. As seen in Scout's treatment of Boo in the final scene, the reward for rethinking one's understanding of these concepts is the chance to truly see the world from another's point of view. In that way, the novel offers powerful lessons about the possibility of moving beyond the superficial differences that divide society.

Notes

Introduction: Enduring Appeal

1. Quoted in Claudia Durst Johnson, To Kill a Mockingbird: *Threatening Boundaries*. New York: Twayne, 1994, p. 21.

Chapter 1: The Life of Harper Lee

2. Harper Lee, foreword to *To Kill a Mockingbird*, thirty-fifth anniversary ed., by Harper Lee. New York: HarperCollins, 1995. http://mockingbird.chebucto.org.

3. Marianne Moates, *A Bridge of Childhood: Truman Capote's Southern Years*. New York: Henry Holt, 1989, pp. 1–2.

4. Marie Rudisill with James C. Simmons, *Truman Capote*. New York: Morrow, 1983, p. 190.

5. Moates, *A Bridge of Childhood*, p. 37.

6. Quoted in Jane Kansas, "*To Kill a Mockingbird*—Roy Newquist Interviews Harper Lee." http://mockingbird.chebucto.org.

7. George Thomas Jones, "She Was the 'Queen of the Tomboys.'" www.educeth.ch/english/readinglist/leeh/remin.html.

8. Rudisill with Simmons, *Truman Capote*, p. 191.

9. Rudisill with Simmons, *Truman Capote*, p. 192.

10. Gloria Steinem, "'Go Right Ahead and Ask Me Anything' (and So She Did): An Interview with Truman Capote," *McCall's*, November 1967, p. 77.

11. Moates, *A Bridge of Childhood*, p. 2.

12. Harper Lee, "Christmas to Me," *McCall's*, December 1961. http://mockingbird.chebucto.org.

13. Tay Hohoff, "We Get a New Author," Introduction to *To Kill a Mockingbird* by Harper Lee. New York: Literary Guild, 1960, p. 3.

14. Tay Hohoff, "We Get a New Author," p. 3.

15. Quoted in Kansas, "*To Kill a Mockingbird*—Roy Newquist Interview Harper Lee."

16. Kathy Kemp, "The Elusive—but Still Alive—Harper Lee," *South-Coast Today*, November 2, 1997. www.southcoasttoday.com.

17. Quoted in George Plimpton, "The Story Behind the Nonfiction Novel," in Thomas M. Inge, ed., *Truman Capote: Conversations.* Jackson: University of Mississippi Press, 1987, p. 52.

18. Truman Capote, *In Cold Blood.* New York: Vintage, 1993.

19. Drew Jubera, "'Mockingbird' Still Sings Despite Silence of Author Harper Lee," *Atlanta Journal,* August 26, 1990, p. M/11.

20. Rheta Grimsley Johnson, "Isn't Writing One Classic Novel Enough?" *Atlanta Constitution,* May 23, 1993, p. A/11.

Chapter 2: Historical Background of the Novel

21. Harper Lee, *To Kill a Mockingbird.* New York: Warner Books, 1982, p. 21.

22. Lee, *To Kill a Mockingbird,* p. 248.

23. Lee, *To Kill a Mockingbird,* p. 119.

24. Quoted in Claudia Durst Johnson, *Understanding* To Kill a Mockingbird: *A Student Casebook to Issues, Sources, and Historical Documents.* Westport, CT: Greenwood Press, 1994, p. 174.

25. Johnson, *"To Kill Mockingbird,"* p. 17.

26. Quoted in Johnson, *Understanding* To Kill a Mockingbird, p. 32.

27. Lee, *To Kill a Mockingbird,* p. 205.

28. Johnson, To Kill a Mockingbird, p. 105.

29. Carolyn Jones, "The Mad Dog as Symbol," in Terry O'Neill, ed., *Readings on* To Kill a Mockingbird. San Diego: Greenhaven, 2000, p. 34.

30. Quoted in Johnson, *"To Kill a Mockingbird,"* p. 16.

31. Jill P. May, "Censors as Critics: *To Kill a Mockingbird* as a Case Study," in *Cross-Culturalism in Children's Literature: Selected Papers from the Children's Literature Association.* New York: Pace University Press, 1998, p. 91.

32. Quoted in Johnson, *Understanding* To Kill a Mockingbird, p. 205.

33. Quoted in Johnson, *Understanding* To Kill a Mockingbird, p. 215.

Chapter 3: The Plot

34. Lee, *To Kill a Mockingbird*, p. 21.
35. Lee, *To Kill a Mockingbird*, p. 27.
36. Lee, *To Kill a Mockingbird*, p. 30.
37. Lee, *To Kill a Mockingbird*, p. 58.
38. Lee, *To Kill a Mockingbird*, p. 74.
39. Lee, *To Kill a Mockingbird*, p. 76.
40. Lee, *To Kill a Mockingbird*, p. 83.
41. Lee, *To Kill a Mockingbird*, p. 270.
42. Lee, *To Kill a Mockingbird*, p. 276.

Chapter 4: The Cast of Characters

43. Lee, *To Kill a Mockingbird*, p. 129.
44. Lee, *To Kill a Mockingbird*, p. 42.
45. Lee, *To Kill a Mockingbird*, p. 112.
46. Lee, *To Kill a Mockingbird*, p. 75.
47. Lee, *To Kill a Mockingbird*, p. 146.
48. Lee, *To Kill a Mockingbird*, p. 205.
49. Jones, "The Mad Dog as Symbol," p. 47.
50. Johnson, To Kill a Mockingbird, p. 102.
51. Lee, *To Kill a Mockingbird*, p. 247.
52. Lee, *To Kill a Mockingbird*, p. 244.
53. Lee, *To Kill a Mockingbird*, p. 247.
54. Lee, *To Kill a Mockingbird*, p. 200.
55. Lee, *To Kill a Mockingbird*, p. 276.

Chapter 5: Literary Criticism

56. Edgar Schuster, "Discovering Theme and Structure in the Novel," in Harold Bloom, ed., *Modern Critical Interpretations: "To Kill a Mockingbird."* Bromhall, PA: Chelsea House, 1998, p. 15.
57. Lee, *To Kill a Mockingbird*, p. 30.
58. Johnson, To Kill a Mockingbird, p. 59.
59. Lee, *To Kill a Mockingbird*, p. 194.

60. Lee, *To Kill a Mockingbird*, pp. 131–2.

61. Lee, *To Kill a Mockingbird*, p. 90.

62. Lee, *To Kill a Mockingbird*, p. 241.

63. Lee, *To Kill a Mockingbird*, p. 276.

64. Lee, *To Kill a Mockingbird*, p. 35.

65. Lee, *To Kill a Mockingbird*, p. 24.

66. Lee, *To Kill a Mockingbird*, p. 108.

67. Lee, *To Kill a Mockingbird*, p. 124.

68. R.A. Dave, "*To Kill a Mockingbird:* Harper Lee's Tragic Vision," in Harold Bloom, ed., *Modern Critical Interpretations:* To Kill a Mockingbird. Bromhall, PA: Chelsea House, 1998, p. 53.

69. Lee, *To Kill a Mockingbird*, p. 208.

70. Lee, *To Kill a Mockingbird*, p. 157.

71. Schuster, "Discovering Theme and Structure in the Novel," p. 10.

72. Lee, *To Kill a Mockingbird*, p. 18.

73. Lee, *To Kill a Mockingbird*, pp. 32–3.

74. Schuster, "Discovering Theme and Structure in the Novel," p. 10.

75. Lee, *To Kill a Mockingbird*, p. 279.

76. Johnson, To Kill a Mockingbird, pp. 96–7.

77. Lee, *To Kill a Mockingbird*, p. 88.

78. Jones, "The Mad Dog as Symbol," p. 41.

79. Lee, *To Kill a Mockingbird*, p. 205.

80. Lee, *To Kill a Mockingbird,* p. 241.

81. Johnson, To Kill a Mockingbird, p. 106.

For Further Exploration

1. Watch the Academy Award–winning film version of *To Kill a Mockingbird*. What happens to the first-person narration in the film? Do you think this was a practical or artistic choice? Why do you think the filmmakers chose to put greater emphasis on Jem's point of view, and how is the story affected as a result? See Colin Nicholson's essay in Bloom, ed., *Modern Critical Interpretations*, pp. 89–98; and Dean Shackelford, "The Female Voice in *To Kill a Mockingbird:* Narrative Strategies in Film and Novel," pp. 115–126.

2. At first glance, Chapter 10, which includes the episode of Atticus shooting a mad dog, may seem disconnected from the trial plot and even the novel as a whole. What is the symbolism of the mad dog? How does this chapter lead to new understanding into Atticus's character? In what ways is the mad dog incident similar to Tom Robinson's trial? See Carolyn Jones, "Atticus Finch and the Mad Dog: Harper Lee's *To Kill a Mockingbird.*"

3. Atticus Finch is a memorable character who is held up as the moral compass of the novel. Many critics, however, debate Atticus's heroism. Do you believe Atticus is indeed a hero? What makes him one—his impassioned defense of a doomed black man, his moral values, or his open-mindedness? What other qualities? Or do you believe Atticus simply accepted the case that was assigned to him and is not necessarily worthy of the hero badge? Why? See Michael Asimov's and Monroe Freedman's chapters in O'Neill, ed., *Readings on* To Kill a Mockingbird, pp. 93–99 and pp. 117–120.

4. In many ways, *To Kill a Mockingbird* is a story about change. Scout and Jem grow up and must incorporate new experiences into their understanding of the world. What aspects of the story remain the same, though? What aspects of the story do you feel still hold true today? See R.A. Dave's essay in Bloom, ed., *Modern Critical Interpretations*, pp. 49–60.

5. Why doesn't Atticus ever tell his children that he was assigned by Judge Taylor to defend Tom Robinson? In what ways does Scout's discovery of this information change her opinion of her father? Does knowing that Atticus was appointed change your opinion of him? See Claudia Durst Johnson, *Understanding* To Kill a Mockingbird.

6. *To Kill a Mockingbird* is divided into two distinct parts. The first part focuses mostly on the children and their attempts to make Boo Radley come out of his house, while the second focuses on the trial of Tom Robinson. How are the two parts related to one another? Why might Harper Lee have chosen to structure her novel this way? See Edgar Schuster's essay in Bloom, ed., *Modern Critical Interpretations*, pp. 7–16; and Claudia Durst Johnson, *Understanding* To Kill a Mockingbird.

7. Compare and contrast the female characters Aunt Alexandra and Miss Maudie Attkinson. What lessons does Scout learn from each about being a woman in the 1930s? See Dean Shackelford, "The Female Voice in *To Kill a Mockingbird:* Narrative Strategies in Film and Novel."

8. During his cross-examination of Mayella Ewell, Atticus tries to get her to admit that she is lying about what happened with Tom Robinson. What do you think would have happened if Mayella had indeed admitted that she made up the entire story? Would the trial have continued? Would the jury still have found Tom guilty? Why or why not? See Claudia Durst Johnson, To Kill a Mockingbird: *Threatening Boundaries.*

9. Read Mark Twain's *Huckleberry Finn,* which also tells the story of growing up in the Deep South and offers profound lessons on race relations. How are the two stories similar? Are the lessons Scout learns the same as those Huck learns? What similarities and differences are there between Tom Robinson and Jim? Are the two authors' visions of life in the Southern United States similar or different? See Fred Erisman's essay in Bloom, ed., *Modern Critical Interpretations,* pp. 39–148.

10. Since the book was published, there have been many attempts to censor To Kill a Mockingbird, particularly to keep it out of some public schools and libraries. Why would some people want to censor this novel? Do you think such censorship attempts are appropriate? Why or why not? See Claudia Durst Johnson, *Understanding* To Kill a Mockingbird.

Appendix of Criticism

Reviews

A Brilliant First Novel

Author Lee, 34, an Alabamian, has written her first novel with all the tactile brilliance and none of the preciosity generally supposed to be standard swamp-warfare issue of Southern writers. The novel is an account of an awakening to good and evil, and a faint catechistic flavor may have been inevitable. But it is faint indeed; novelist Lee's prose has an edge that cuts through cant, and she teaches the reader an astonishing number of useful truths about little girls and about Southern life. (A notable one: "Naming people after Confederate generals makes slow steady drinkers.") All in all, Scout Finch is fiction's most appealing child since Carson McCullers' Frankie got left behind at the wedding.

> Excerpted from a review in the August 1, 1960, issue of *Time*.

Opposing Themes Take Away from the Graceful Writing of Lee's First Novel

In her first novel, *To Kill a Mockingbird*, Harper Lee makes a valiant attempt to combine two dominant themes of contemporary Southern fiction—the recollection of childhood among village eccentrics and the spirit-corroding shame of the civilized white Southerner in the treatment of the Negro. If her attempt fails to produce a novel of stature, or even of original insight, it does provide an exercise in easy, graceful writing and some genuinely moving and mildly humorous excursions into the transient world of childhood. . . .

The two themes Miss Lee interweaves throughout the novel emerge as enemies of each other. The charm and wistful humor of the childhood recollections do not foreshadow the deeper, harsher note which pervades the later pages of the book. The Negro, the poor white girl who victimizes him, and the wretched community spirit that defeats him, never rise in definition to match the eccentric, vagrant, and appealing characters with which the story opens. The two worlds remain solitary in spite of Miss Lee's grace of writing and honorable decency of intent.

> Excerpted from Harding LeMay, "Children Play; Adults Betray," *New York Herald Tribune Book Review*, July 10, 1960.

Child's Perspective Is Unconvincing

Harper Lee's *To Kill a Mockingbird* gives a friendly but for the most part unsentimental account of life in an Alabama town in the 1930s. The narrator, Jean Louise (commonly called Scout) Finch, is writing of a time when she was seven or eight years old, and the book is in part the record of a childhood. Their mother being dead, Scout and her brother Jem have been brought up by their father, a lawyer and legislator, and by a Negro servant, Calpurnia. The father, Atticus Finch, is an unusual man, and their childhood is in many ways a unique one.

Miss Lee, however, is not primarily concerned with childhood experience; she has, in her own way, written a novel about the perennial Southern problem. Atticus is assigned to defend a Negro charged with raping a white woman, and, to the dismay of his neighbors, he really tries to defend him. Through Scout's eyes we watch the growth of resentment in the community and then we see the trial itself, in which Atticus is inevitably defeated. After that there is a melodramatic conclusion.

Miss Lee's problem has been to tell the story she wants to tell and yet to stay within the consciousness of a child, and she hasn't consistently solved it. Some episodes in the trial and the melodramatic conclusion seem contrived. But her insight into Southern mores is impressive, and in Atticus she has done a notable portrait of a Southern liberal.

Excerpted from Granville Hicks, "Three at the Outset,"
Saturday Review, July 23, 1960.

Literary Criticism

Atticus Finch Is Novel's Moral Center

The deepest symbol in the novel is Atticus Finch himself. Atticus, when he gives his children their air rifles, states the moral lesson of the novel. He tells them that it is a sin to kill a mockingbird; that is, it is wrong to do harm to something or to someone who only tries to help us or to give us pleasure. That rule, combined with critical reflection on the self and with compassion for others, keeps us from becoming mad dogs, from destroying each other, and, finally, ourselves. Scout understands this lesson as she, along with Sheriff Heck Tate and her father, argue that Boo should not be charged for Bob Ewell's murder. When Atticus asks Scout if she understands this adult decision, she responds: "Well, it'd be sort of like shootin' a mockingbird, wouldn't it?"

Atticus stands at the novel's heart and as its moral and ethical center: a man who knows himself and who, therefore, can love others.

Scout presents her father to us as a gift and a guide. She shows us a man who gives up himself, yet is far from being a "grey ghost." Atticus emerges clearly, as a particular, ethical human being . . . but also as an enduring symbol of the good.

Excerpted from Carolyn Jones, "Atticus Finch and the Mad Dog: Harper Lee's *To Kill a Mockingbird*," *Southern Quarterly*, Summer 1996.

Lessons About Gender Roles

To Scout, Atticus and his world represent freedom and power. Atticus is the key representative of the male power which Scout wishes to obtain even though she is growing up as a Southern female. More important, Lee demonstrates that Scout is gradually becoming a feminist in the South, for, with the use of first-person narration, she indicates that Scout/Jean Louise still maintains the ambivalence about being a Southern lady she possessed as a child. She seeks to become empowered with the freedoms the men in her society seem to possess without question and without resorting to trivial and superficial concerns such as wearing a dress and appearing genteel.

Harper Lee's fundamental criticism of gender roles for women (and to a lesser extent for men) may be evident especially in her novel's identification with outsider figures such as Tom Robinson, Mayella Ewell, and Boo Radley. Curiously enough, the outsider figures with whom the novelist identifies most are also males. Tom Robinson, the male African American who has been disempowered and annihilated by a fundamentally racist, white male society, and Boo Radley, the reclusive and eccentric neighbor about whom legends of his danger to the fragile Southern society circulate regularly, are the two "mockingbirds" of the title. Ironically, they are unable to mock society's roles for them and as a result take the consequences of living on the margins—Tom, through his death; Boo, through his return to the protection of a desolate isolated existence.

Throughout the novel, however, the female voice has emphasized Scout's growing distance from her provincial Southern society and her identification with her father, a symbol of the empowered. Like her father, Atticus, Scout, too, is unable to be a "mockingbird" of society and as a result, in coming to know Boo Radley as a real human being at novel's end, she recognizes the empowerment of being the other as she consents to remain an outsider unable to accept society's unwillingness to seek and know before it judges.

Excerpted from Dean Shackelford, "The Female Voice in *To Kill a Mockingbird:* Narrative Strategies in Film and Novel," *Mississippi Quarterly*, Winter 1996/97.

Novel Offers Lessons on Overcoming Difference

The success of *To Kill a Mockingbird*, one of the most frequently read novels of the last hundred years, can be attributed to its powerful, universal themes. One central theme, encompassing both Part One (which is primarily Boo Radley's story) and Part Two (which is primarily Tom Robinson's story), is that valuable lessons are learned in confronting those who are unlike ourselves and unlike those we know best—what might be called people of difference. In the story, the children must grow up, learn civilizing truths, and rise above the narrowness of the place and time in which private codes and even some legal practices contradict the idealistic principles that the community professes: "Equal rights for all, special privileges for none," as Scout says. In practice, however, equal justice was not available to Boo Radley at that turning point in his life; nor is it available to the Tom Robinsons of this world.

Within such a social climate, the children learn how citizens of their community, which is made up of different races, classes, and temperaments, interact in times of crisis. The "outsiders" in this novel are primarily represented by the unseen eccentric, Boo Radley, and by the African-American, Tom Robinson. They are clearly outside the mainstream of Maycomb society, even though they have lived in the community for as long as most can remember. Because of their position in society, they are at first regarded by the children as demonic and witchlike. But in the process of maturing, the children come to embrace the outsiders among them. Even more, they come to acknowledge their kinship with outsiders—in a sense, the outsider within themselves.

Excerpted from Claudia Durst Johnson, *Understanding* To Kill a Mockingbird: *A Student Casebook to Issues, Sources, and Historical Documents*. Westport, CT: Greenwood Press, 1994.

Lee Incorporates Autobiographical Material into *To Kill a Mockingbird*

To Kill a Mockingbird is autobiographical not merely in most of its expression but also in quite a personal sense. . . . Jean Louise Finch (Scout) is unmistakably Harper Lee. If we examine the internal evidence, we can easily infer that in 1935, while Hitler was persecuting the Jews in Germany and Tom Robinson was being tried in Maycomb, Jean "Scout" Finch, the narrator, was "not yet nine," perhaps she was born, like her creator, in 1926. The identification between the narrator and the novelist is apparent. The novel with its autobiographical mode strikes a balance between the past, the present, and the future. The writer projects herself into the story as Scout in the present. What she narrates is in the past. And as the past is unfolded the reader wonders how the writer's retrospect will lead her on to the future, which is a continual mystery. This evokes in the novel considerable suspense. We follow the trial of Tom Robinson and the ostracizing of the Finch family, holding our breath.

> Excerpted from R.A. Dave's essay in Harold Bloom, ed., *Modern Critical Interpretations:* To Kill a Mockingbird. Bromhall, PA: Chelsea House, 1998.

Illegal Channels Ultimately Prove More Just than "Higher Law"

In short, in the dark hour of the novel, Atticus's higher law is an ineffective defense against Bob Ewell's chaos, as useless as facing a mad dog in the street without a gun. Only a miracle, some *deus ex machina*, in this case Boo Radley, can overcome chaos. Even a humane and civilized system of law becomes at some point, and under certain circumstances, severely limited when primitive, hidden codes or lawlessness merge so powerfully. In the case of Boo Radley's killing of Bob Ewell, law is proven inadequate for another reason, because on occasion laws must be overridden for justice to be done. Circumstance must override honor; an individual human being's needs must supercede principle. Ewell's death must be reported as an accidental suicide instead of as a homicide. It is not a step that Atticus takes lightly. . . . But Atticus has always been more insistent that he and his own strong kind obey a higher law (pulling them up on the evolutionary ladder) than the weak Ewells and Cunninghams. Only when he finds out that it is not Jem but Boo who has killed Bob Ewell does he relent to the secrecy that will circumvent a legal hearing. For Atticus knows Boo to be "one of the least of these," as scripture delineates the earth's dispossessed, those who stand in for Christ. In a final act that secures Atticus's sainthood, he momentarily, hesitantly relinquishes for Boo Radley's sake what is more sacred to him, the code he lives by.

> Excerpted from Claudia Durst Johnson, To Kill a Mockingbird: *Threatening Boundaries.* New York: Twayne, 1994.

Chronology

1926
Nelle Harper Lee is born in Monroeville, Alabama, on April 28.

1928–1939
Truman Capote, the future writer, spends summers living next door to the Lees.

1929
The stock market crashes, marking the beginning of the economic Great Depression that will last ten years.

1931
In Scottsboro, Alabama, nine black men are brought to trial when two white women falsely accuse them of rape. The men are found guilty and sentenced to death, and the case goes through several rounds of appeals over the next twenty years. The last of the defendants is finally released in 1950.

1944–1945
Lee attends Huntingdon College, a women's college in Montgomery, Alabama.

1945–1950
Lee transfers to the University of Alabama, where she studies law, as her father did. She drops out before completing the degree, however.

1948
Truman Capote publishes his first novel, *Other Voices, Other Rooms.* The character of Idabell is loosely based on Lee.

1950
Lee moves to New York City, where she spends her days working as an airline reservation clerk and her evenings writing.

1951
Lee's mother dies.

1954
In the historic *Brown* v. *Board of Education* case, the U.S. Supreme Court declares segregated schools are unconstitutional.

1955

A major event in the burgeoning civil rights movement takes place in Alabama. Rosa Parks, a black woman, refuses to move to the back of a public bus per segregation law.

1956

Lee's friends give her a large monetary Christmas gift so she can quit her job for a year and devote herself full-time to writing. Autherine Lucy, a young black college student, attempts to enroll at the University of Alabama. U.S. courts rule the college must admit her, but violent student protests force Lucy to leave.

1957

Lee finishes her draft of *To Kill Mockingbird*. Tay Hohoff, an editor at J.B. Lippincott, expresses interest in the manuscript and helps Lee revise it for publication. After protests in Little Rock, Arkansas, federal troops are sent in to enforce court-ordered desegregation of schools.

1959

Lee accompanies Capote on several trips to research his forthcoming book *In Cold Blood*, a major documentary novel about the murder of a Kansas family and the execution of their killers.

1960

To Kill a Mockingbird is published. It moves to the best-seller list and stays there for eighty weeks.

1961

Lee is awarded the Pulitzer prize for *To Kill a Mockingbird*, the first woman honored with the award since 1942. She publishes two short essays: "Christmas to Me" in the December issue of *McCall's* and "Love—In Other Words" in the April *Vogue*. Lee begins work on a second novel, which is never published. Her father dies.

1962

To Kill a Mockingbird is adapted into an Academy Award–winning film. Lee is awarded an honorary degree from Mount Holyoke, a prestigious women's college in Massachusetts.

1963

The tumultuous civil rights movement continues. President John F. Kennedy is assassinated.

1965
Martin Luther King Jr. leads civil rights demonstrators on a peaceful protest march across Alabama. Capote's *In Cold Blood* is published, with a dedication to Lee. Lee publishes "When Children Discover America" in the August issue of *McCall's*.

1966
Lee is appointed by President Lyndon Johnson to the National Council of the Arts.

1968
Martin Luther King Jr. is assassinated.

1970
To Kill a Mockingbird is adapted into a successful stage production by playwright Christopher Sergel.

1990
Lee receives an honorary degree from the University of Alabama.

1995
Thirty-fifth anniversary edition of *To Kill a Mockingbird* is published, with a short foreword by Lee. A *New York Times* reporter later reveals the foreword is actually a letter from Lee to her agent, requesting the book *not* be published with a new introduction.

2000–present
Lee splits her time between New York City and Monroeville, where she lives with her sister. She lives a reclusive life, refusing all interviews and nearly all awards.

Works Consulted

Major Editions of *To Kill a Mockingbird*

Harper Lee, *To Kill a Mockingbird*. New York: J.B. Lippincott, 1960.

Harper Lee, *To Kill a Mockingbird*. New York: Literary Guild, 1960.

Harper Lee, *To Kill a Mockingbird*. New York: Popular Library, 1962. Published as a tie-in to the film version.

Harper Lee, *To Kill a Mockingbird*. New York: Warner Books, 1982. [edition used for reference in this book]

Harper Lee, *To Kill a Mockingbird*. New York: HarperCollins, 1995. Special thirty-fifth anniversary edition, which includes a new "foreword" by Lee.

Also by Harper Lee

"Christmas to Me," *McCall's*, December 1961. It tells the story of Lee receiving a monetary Christmas gift from friends so she can take a year to devote to writing full-time.

"Love—In Other Words," *Vogue*, April 15, 1961, a short article concerning Lee's thoughts on nonromantic love.

"When Children Discover America," *McCall's*, August 1965. In this piece, Lee argues why children should learn about the United States at an early age.

Biographies

Marianne Moates, *A Bridge of Childhood: Truman Capote's Southern Years*. New York: Henry Holt, 1989. A biography of Capote written by a former Monroeville resident, it includes details on Capote's childhood growing up with Lee.

Marie Rudisill with James C. Simmons, *Truman Capote*. New York: Morrow, 1983. Capote's aunt wrote this unauthorized biography shortly before his death. With no full-length biography of Lee, this work provides the most detailed account of Lee's childhood.

Literary Reviews and Criticism

Harold Bloom, ed., *Modern Critical Interpretations: "To Kill a Mockingbird."* Bromhall, PA: Chelsea House, 1998. A collection of critical essays and reviews, edited by renowned Yale professor Harold Bloom.

Truman Capote, *In Cold Blood*. New York: Vintage, 1993. Truman Capote's famous book, first published in 1966, was the first in the true crime genre.

William T. Going, "Store and Mockingbird: Two Pulitzer Novels About Alabama," in *Essays on Alabama Literature*. Tuscaloosa: University of Alabama Press, 1975. Comparison of Lee's novel to T.S. Stribling's *The Store*, the 1934 Pulitzer prize winner.

Granville Hicks, "Three at the Outset," *Saturday Review*, July 23, 1960. An early review that criticizes Lee's choice for Jean Louise to tell the story through the eyes of her childhood self.

Claudia Durst Johnson, To Kill a Mockingbird: *Threatening Boundaries*. New York: Twayne, 1994. The only full-length scholarly text devoted entirely to Lee's novel.

Claudia Durst Johnson, *Understanding* To Kill a Mockingbird: *A Student Casebook to Issues, Sources, and Historical Documents*. Westport, CT: Greenwood Press, 1994. Contains primary sources to help students better understand the novel's historical and sociological context.

Rheta Grimsley Johnson, "Isn't Writing One Classic Novel Enough?" *Atlanta Constitution*, May 23, 1993. Johnson wonders why people question why Lee wrote only one book, noting that when one writes a brilliant book as she did, it would be difficult to top.

Carolyn Jones, "Atticus Finch and the Mad Dog: Harper Lee's *To Kill a Mockingbird*," *Southern Quarterly*, Summer 1996. A discussion of the literal and figurative "mad dogs" in the novel.

George Thomas Jones, "She Was the 'Queen of the Tomboys.'" www.educeth.ch. A former classmate of Lee's remembers the author as a child in this short article.

Drew Jubera, "'Mockingbird' Still Sings Despite Silence of Author Harper Lee," *Atlanta Journal*, August 26, 1990, p. M/11. Short article that describes Lee's reluctance to speak publicly about her novel.

Jane Kansas, To Kill a Mockingbird, http://mockingbird.chebucto.org. A website filled with all kinds of resources about the novel, Lee, and the historical background. Includes Lee's three magazine articles, the full-text of a rare interview, and more.

Kathy Kemp, "The Elusive—but Still Alive—Harper Lee," *SouthCoast Today*, November 2, 1997. An article about one reporter's failed attempts to interview Lee in Monroeville.

Susan King, "How the Finch Stole Christmas: Q & A with Gregory Peck," *Los Angeles Times*, December 22, 1997. An interview with actor Gregory Peck, who won a 1963 Best

Actor Oscar for his portrayal of Atticus Finch in the film version of *To Kill a Mockingbird*.

Harding LeMay, "Children Play; Adults Betray," *New York Herald Tribune Book Review*, July 10, 1960. An early review that argues the two parts of Lee's novel do not complement each other.

Jill P. May, "Censors as Critics: *To Kill a Mockingbird* as a Case Study," in *Cross-Culturalism in Children's Literature: Selected Papers from the Children's Literature Association*. New York: Pace University Press, 1998. Explores the censorship debates surrounding *To Kill a Mockingbird*.

Leigh Montgomery, "Harper Lee Still Prizes Privacy Over Publicity," *Christian Science Monitor*, September 11, 1997. Brief article discussing Lee's aversion to life in the limelight.

Roy Newquist, *Counterpoint*. New York: Rand McNally, 1964. Collection of interviews, which includes one of the only published interviews with Lee.

Terry O'Neill, ed., *Readings on* To Kill a Mockingbird. San Diego: Greenhaven, 2000. A useful collection of critical and historical essays, including a piece on censorship and the novel and debate on Atticus Finch's status as hero.

George Plimpton, "The Story Behind the Nonfiction Novel," in Thomas M. Inge, ed., *Truman Capote: Conversations*. Jackson: University of Mississippi Press, 1987. In this interview, Capote talks about work on his novel *In Cold Blood* and Lee's role in helping him research it.

Dean Shackelford, "The Female Voice in *To Kill a Mockingbird*: Narrative Strategies in Film and Novel," *Mississippi Quarterly*, Winter 1996/97. Comparison of the emphasis on gender roles in the film and novel.

Gloria Steinem, "'Go Right Ahead and Ask Me Anything' (and So She Did): An Interview with Truman Capote," *McCall's*, November 1967. An interview with Capote after the publication of *In Cold Blood*.

W.J. Stuckey, *Pulitzer Prize Novels: A Critical Look Backward*. Norman: University of Oklahoma Press, 1966. Includes a lukewarm discussion of Lee's novel.

Mary B.W. Tabor, "A 'New Foreword' That Isn't," *New York Times*, August 23, 1995. Explains that the new foreword to the thirty-fifth anniversary edition is actually a letter Lee wrote in 1993 expressly asking that her novel not be reissued with an introduction.

Historical Context

Dan Carter, *Scottsboro: A Tragedy of the American South.* Baton Rouge: Louisiana State University Press, 1979. One of the few full-length texts devoted to the Scottsboro trials.

Wayne Flint, *Poor but Proud: Alabama's Poor White.* Tuscaloosa: University of Alabama Press, 1989. Argues against the image of poor white Southerners as immoral, unemployed "trash."

Henry Hampton and Steve Fayer, with Sarah Flynn, *Voices of Freedom: An Oral History of the Civil Rights Movement from the 1950s Through the 1980s.* New York: Bantam Books, 1990. A collection of memories of the major events of the civil rights movement, told from notable people who lived through it.

Doug Linder, "Without Fear or Favor: Judge Horton and the Scottsboro Boys," www.law.umkc.edu. Provides historical background on the Scottsboro case, including primary documents.

Index

Picture Credits

About the Author

Catherine Bernard works as an editor in New York. She received her B.A. in English and French from Rutgers University and her M.A. in English from Columbia University. She has written several other non-fiction books for young adults, including one about Celtic mythology. Catherine likes to travel and has studied abroad in France and Italy. Currently, she lives in New Jersey with her husband and their cat.